Under the **Social Influence**

"I instruct my staff each year before our annual trade show that they are all actors in a play. Each member of the staff has their own role to play on the stage. There are thousands of eyes on them and, until they have pulled their car into their garages at home, they are to be 'in character.' Eye contact, smiles, appearance, and attitudes are very important in our line of work. Under the Social Influence will be an excellent tool for me to share with my new Millennial staff members. The plain-spoken way in which the content is delivered and the personal experiences will go a long way in training somebody just entering the job market. My college freshman son is definitely getting this book as a stocking stuffer this Christmas!"

Don Gilpin, COO, Custom Electronic Design
& Installation Association (CEDIA)

"What a good read! Chuck's book provides valuable 'life lessons' to all who aspire to start a career, as well as to those of us who have been fortunate enough to become successful. Workforce development through teaching skills and mentoring to imprint values and work ethic is critical to the future success of any business, while understanding the 'rules of work' is critical to an individual's workplace success. In addition, Chuck artfully points out how finding and practicing balance in our lives outside work is critical to our happiness. This book offers a step-by-step guide, and the questions at the end of each chapter are spot-on for self-evaluation."

Kerry Moyer, Chairman, Electronic
Systems Professional Alliance (ESPA)

"Once I started reading this book, I couldn't put it down. Under the Social Influence crystallizes the parallels between parenting and employing so clearly that it's obvious the author has done both. As I read it, all too often I found myself introspective and sometimes in conflict with the methods of both my parenting and my managing. This book presents the absolute truth about the seemingly unending social pressures facing the next generation workforce. Every young person (most certainly both of our children) need to read and digest this book's message and its mantra. I plan to make it 'required reading' for all current and future employees. Kudos, Chuck, for taking the risk and bringing it all to light."

Ron Pusey, President & CEO, CSI of VA

"For over three decades I have always had a new business book at my side. It's part of my informal personal improvement process, the result of my Catholic boarding school discipline and the sports programs I experienced for twelve years. Most of what I read goes in the trash can or is erased from my Kindle. The good books are passed to friends and business associates. The really valuable books, with life messages, are passed on to my children. This is my acid test, and I will make sure my girls read Chuck's book cover to cover. Chuck Wilson's book is not always politically correct, but it is honest and built on life experiences that can truly help an open young mind."

Bill Bozeman, President & CEO, PSA Security Network

"Chuck Wilson is one of the most honest people I've ever met. It has been an honor to know him professionally and socially for the past thirty years. In his new book, Under the Social Influence, Chuck clearly describes all the foolish things we've done and how we set ourselves up to do them. All smart, aspiring, young people, as well as myself, can use Chuck's thirty years of real-time research to help perpetuate our industry. In his book, Chuck says, 'One day you will learn that the greatest obstacle to your success will be your own fear…primarily the fear of taking a chance and failing.' No statement could be more true, and we can all learn so much from reading this book. I will use it as an instruction manual and for online training. I'm so proud to support our industry, its members, and organizations like the NSCA Education Foundation."

Loyd Ivey, CEO, Mitek Corp., and founding
member of the NSCA Education Foundation

"Chuck...You have described the reality of life, both on the personal side and the business side of the equation, in a way that is understandable to all sectors of the populace. This will undoubtedly become a 'must-read' for all those entering the workforce for the first time, or those of us who are at times struggling to understand the younger generation's daily mindset. Congratulations on a job well done!"

Steve Emspak, global technology consultant

"Plain speaking and common sense are alive and well in Chuck Wilson's book Under the Social Influence. I found myself nodding my head 'yes' time after time as Chuck explained some complex issues in basic and easy-to-understand terms and provided simple, no-nonsense solutions and ideas that anyone can implement if they choose to heed his advice. For any person who is looking to be employed, who is currently employed, or even an employer, this book is a must-read, and I can see how readily it could be implemented as an additional HR resource in any company as a new employee primer or reference book in support of the standard company employment manual. I found that in chapter after chapter I was able to get at least one good idea or thought from Chuck's descriptions. In this day and age of politically correct literature, I found Chuck's book to be rewarding and refreshing in its honest and common-sense approach to issues within the workplace and in life generally."

Andrew Musci, President/CEO, Altel Systems, Inc.

"Under the Social Influence takes the reader back to the basics of a balanced life. It causes one to consider altering the old saying, 'The more things change, the more they stay the same,' to 'The more things change, the more they need to stay the same.' I found this book to be a wonderful reminder of the basic concepts of a successful life that are constant. Readers of this book would do well to answer the questions at the end of each chapter and do a little soul searching. Sometimes the simple ideas can take us the furthest. Taking responsibility for one's own life can never start too early."

Mike Bradley, business leader

"If the US economy is going to continue to remain the most productive in the world, we're going to have learn how to bridge the needs and motivations of multiple generations like never before in our history. That's a pretty monumental task! But after reading this book, I see a pathway to success, whether you're a giant multinational company or a small entrepreneur trying to make a mark."

Todd Thibodeaux, President and CEO, CompTIA

Under the
Social
Influence

*Going From Reckless to Responsible
in Today's Socially Distracted Society*

Chuck Wilson

NEW YORK

Under the **Social Influence**
Going From Reckless to Responsible in Today's Socially Distracted Society

ISBN 978-1-61448-465-3 paperback
ISBN 978-1-61448-466-0 eBook
Library of Congress Control Number: 2012935391

Morgan James Publishing
The Entrepreneurial Publisher
5 Penn Plaza, 23rd Floor,
New York City, New York 10001
(212) 655-5470 office • (516) 908-4496 fax
www.MorganJamesPublishing.com

Cover Design by:
Rachel Lopez
www.r2cdesign.com

Interior Design by:
Bonnie Bushman
bonnie@caboodlegraphics.com

In an effort to support local communities, raise awareness and funds, Morgan James Publishing donates a percentage of all book sales for the life of each book to Habitat for Humanity Peninsula and Greater Williamsburg.

Get involved today, visit
www.MorganJamesBuilds.com.

Habitat
for Humanity®
Peninsula and
Greater Williamsburg
Building Partner

Almost every word of this book was written while traveling somewhere for business. For each of the last sixteen years I've spent on average 125 days away from home. Because of this, I missed about a third of my son's life growing up, and that placed a tremendous burden on my wife at times. The support of my family made it possible to experience all the things I've shared in the book.

I would like to dedicate this work to my wife, Pam, and son, Austin.

Table of Contents

Introduction

We are in the middle of a social revolution. Social media has added another layer of complexity and in many cases has done damage to the reputation of young employees as they build the foundation of a rewarding career. Intense social pressures such as peer influence, political conformity, appearance, and economic strains have dramatically complicated our lives and have become the new normal.

After years of mentoring, coaching, and observing hundreds of technical workers as they began their careers, I've seen this demographic really struggle to get ahead. My industry sector, like most, lacks a playbook that describes the interaction between work and life and importance of a healthy work/life balance.

For example, one of my close friends had an employee that both he and I observed and helped mentor. This well-educated young woman fought a constant battle of social pressures that would eventually unravel every job she ever held. She wanted to be a perfect friend, a perfect mother, and a perfect employee—and still keep her active social life intact. The influences on her life were killing her financially and professionally and causing unnecessary drama in every part of her life. Her mistakes were simple and correctable, and yet she didn't acknowledge any of them. She was her own worst enemy. She was addicted to every social influence possible and valued the opinions of her dysfunctional friends—most of whom were as unhappy as she was.

This story is repeated by thousands of young men and women scrambling to make a decent life for themselves and their families. In this book, I'm going to share with you a more balanced approach to make your life better. In fact, this book may just keep you from getting fired.

Many jobs and professions today require excellent communications and people skills and maintain a traditional office protocol. The Millennial generation (born between the year 1983 and 2001), influenced by reality TV and YouTube video clips, often forget that a critical aspect of sustained employment is professional interaction in the workplace. Many well-educated, extremely intelligent young professionals don't always know how to conduct themselves and how to communicate with peers and managers when they get their first "real" job. Based on thirty years of helping dozens of companies develop organizational structures, design new employee orientation programs, craft position descriptions, and develop mentoring programs, I've found that too many summer, college, and part-time jobs actually become a set up for failure in the vastly different professional business place.

The Baby Boomer generation (born between the year 1946 and 1964) will often have a predisposed bias toward young professionals entering the business world for the first time. They seem to have serious behavioral issues: too many distractions, poor people skills, lack of a work ethic, and no respect for authority. I've discovered that, in many cases, our new workforce has been educated to believe that performance, not behavior, matters. This is far from the truth. Behavior does matter, as does a genuinely nice personality. There simply are right and wrong approaches to workplace communication, behavior, performance, and attitude—and if you want to keep your job, you must learn the difference.

The problem: While many people new to the workforce are more technologically savvy than ever, they are dismally ill-equipped to handle face-to-face business interactions. I'm a strong believer that members of this generation, with proper guidance, will become wildly successful when they find a job that they can be passionate about and that will continually pique their interest. I want to help them succeed by showing them how technology can be merged into human interaction without replacing it.

I've been extremely blessed and very fortunate to have been around many great mentors and business leaders in my career that have taught me a lot about how to truly change lives for the better—at work and at home. One of the great things about producing events and conferences around the world is that I've been able to hear some of the best presenters, inspirational speakers, political figures, sport and music legends, motivational speakers, and business leaders.

I've drawn my insight from meeting people with great stories of overcoming adversity. Montel Williams, who suffers from multiple sclerosis yet keeps on going, and Rulon Gardner, who nearly died twice in separate incidents and also keeps on, are just two examples. I've visited with Colin Powell and

George H.W. Bush, learning from them to appreciate what real stress is about and how they leaned on their core values to make strategic decisions that impacted the entire world. I've met people who were very successful but difficult to like. Bobby Knight and Mark Cuban—two such people—achieved their success through an unwavering level of intensity and a "winning at any expense" mentality. I spent a day with Jack Canfield, creator of the *Chicken Soup for the Soul* books, and was amazed at the connection between writing and creating the proper work and life balance. I've attended workshops with Rick Warren and Jim Collins, two great authors who provided me with the motivation to help others over the years with the challenges of business.

From these amazing authors, inventors, business leaders, and political figures, I've formed a strong opinion on the best, and sometimes worst, methods for successfully balancing a business and personal life and tying them together successfully. Each of the people knew how to lead others for achieving results. Some did so in a way they could be proud of; others didn't care about the method, just the results.

I've also heard the stories of ordinary people I met on airplanes and of students and entry-level technology employees in various parts of the world. I've gleaned as much from the Millennial generation as I have from the most brilliant minds of my generation (the Baby Boomer generation). Some of these personal stories helped me draw a line between those things I would and wouldn't do to get ahead. In other cases, their messages were spot-on advice for those who struggle to overcome the wrong influences. I've learned from the wildly successful and from those struggling to just get by that the first step toward success is to understand that your home life and work life are inherently connected. When your home life is out of balance, it's going to show up in the form of distractions and mistakes at work, and vice versa. To find success in the long run, your home life and work life must be healthy and fully integrated. Creating balance amidst the chaos while making time for what's most important is very difficult because we no longer disconnect from our technology.

For the younger generation, striving for a balanced life may be easier said than done. Unlike my generation, where most families had two married parents living under the same roof, nearly 55 percent of young Americans today come from "non-traditional" homes. These young professionals now enter the workforce with tremendous technical skills and are well educated, but they often lack basic communication, emotional, or people skills—the "soft" skills that form the foundation of a successful career.

Employers are indeed seeing dysfunctional social habits and poor communications skills negatively affecting work life. The most basic social interactions—vocal and written—are being replaced by electronic messaging, leaving us at a point where we can no longer assume that basic social skills have been ingrained by the family interaction and parental training we have always taken for granted. It's not just about family values, it's the complete breakdown of traditional communications, as conflict resolution has been compromised by the convenience (and avoidance) of sending a text.

The very meaning of "work ethic" has changed, based upon examples set by authority figures. Time and money have different values now too. Working hard and working smart have taken on new meanings. The pride of working for just one or two companies over an entire career has diminished. Trust and loyalty have been redefined by the "what's in it for me" attitude.

In other words, the rising number of single parent homes isn't the only generational difference that's having a big impact on the workplace. Compared to the previous generation, the childrearing practices popular today show a clear absence of what my generation refers to as "tough love." Many researchers have concluded that the hectic schedules of the two-income family have created an absence of teachable moments for parents, leaving preteens and teenagers to gain their wisdom and wit from the Kardashians, Snooki, or Stewie.

The entitlement issue we read so much about isn't necessarily the fault of the Millennial. Parents carry much of the responsibility for over-stimulating their children's senses with constant shuttling to play dates, soccer games, dance lessons, clinics, camps, private lessons, and so on. They have been pampered, celebrated, nurtured, and preprogrammed to believe that rushing from one appointment to the next is the norm and that a career should advance as quickly as did the next level in karate class. Parents want their children to have it all, or at least more than they did growing up. Parents that allow children to join two or three sports at once, to randomly quit a program if they're not excelling, and to argue with coaches over playing time, have instilled a job-hopping mentality in this generation. That is a bad habit for a Millennial and one that needs to be broken quickly upon entering the workforce. If everything came easy for them as children, working hard and being patient for advancement will be very difficult to accept.

In light of all of this, I've concluded that many Millennials are guilty of living and working under the influence—the *social* influence. Being active in social media, having a healthy social life, and socializing with coworkers can all be stressful; how to navigate all of this is almost never taught. In practical terms, you can simplify your life by becoming aware of the most common traps and mistakes, and learning how to avoid them. In other words, you can become more successful by simply being smart, rather than slavishly following what are largely just distractions.

For young people just getting started, my hope is that this book will serve as a primer for beginning your first real job and launching a serious and rewarding career. Here you'll find a compilation of the best methods I've found over the course of my travels and work experiences to successfully balance a business and personal life and tie them together successfully. My hope is that this book can serve as a guide, or dashboard, to show you where you are in terms of finding balance in your life: where you're going, how fast you're going, and especially how close you are to empty. You may find some of the crazy stories about what can happen in the life of a Millennial all too familiar, and I hope you'll see how your social life and your work life affect each other—to determine whether you too are working under the social influence—and how positive changes in one can result in positive changes in the other.

Our workforce is changing faster than my generation is prepared for. The reality is that many older workers who own or manage companies will be staying in these jobs far beyond traditional retirement age. At best these executives are struggling to manage workers who show up in flip-flops, listen to their iPods at their desks, want flexible hours, rapid advancements, and more free time. You want work to be part of your life, not consume it, as you saw with your parents. It should be expected that the traditional structure and chain of command in corporate America will frustrate you. How you choose to deal with it is really up to you.

All this said, this book isn't just for young people; it's also for their mentors and supervisors. I encourage mentorship in the workplace, and I've structured this book so that it can be used for mentoring others. Workforce development is a key to business success, and our research shows that while most employers are pleased with employees' technical skills, what companies want most in their technical workers are better communications skills. As our world becomes more advanced, the technology we provide becomes more software- and application-oriented, but communicating proper usage, providing customer service, support, and user training requires soft skills. Unfortunately, they're not often taught to the next generation of employees.

Each chapter includes an interactive section at the end so you can help young people apply these principles to their own lives and integrate some behavioral corrections to a lifestyle that just isn't working. I strongly believe this book can help shape the careers of the next generation as part of a supportive mentoring relationship. If you aren't already a mentor, I hope you'll consider it. It can truly take your career or influence to the next level.

The chapters that follow offer some suggestions that should help you understand the workplace you are now entering. If you read this book and find nothing that pertains to you, please call your parents and thank them.

PART 1

SIMPLIFY YOUR LIFE: DETERMINE YOUR CORE VALUES

Chapter 1

Reality check: Are you living under the *social* influence?

I s your life overbooked with too many meaningless things as a result of poor time management and not being able to say no? On average we spend more than two hours a day just checking and responding to work e-mail. When you add Facebook and Twitter into the mix, the hours you spend on social media in an effort to stay connected with family and friends does just the opposite: it makes you less social. Have you isolated yourself from people because of your addiction to social media? I see no evidence that the instant connectivity of social networking has made anyone's life simpler or better. I've seen it used as an anonymous and asynchronous way to vent frustration and damage relationships.

Are you obsessed with having more stuff than your friends and setting career goals based strictly upon an income level to support this obsession? Do you feel that life doesn't seem fair? The truth is, life doesn't have to be a constant competition, especially not with friends, neighbors, or family. If it feels that way, then you're experiencing a lot more stress than you really should at your age.

Let's take a quick test of where you are today, and then see how you got there and why. This ten-point checklist is the "misery meter" for those racing to get to an undetermined destination as fast as they possibly can.

How many of these ten statements below describe you?

- ❏ Always late, feeling rushed, frazzled
- ❏ Always angry at someone or about something
- ❏ Always broke and live paycheck to paycheck
- ❏ Always tired, or exhausted, or frustrated
- ❏ Always feel lonely but are seldom alone
- ❏ Always apologizing for underperforming
- ❏ Never face to face with your closest friends
- ❏ Never are happy and seldom laugh at work
- ❏ Never willing to stop the destructive habits
- ❏ Never unplugged from technology

If you checked the majority of the boxes, then your life needs a simplification. From my vantage point, I see far too many young people who are simply overextended in every facet of their lives because of impatience, bad advice, mismanaged finances, and unhealthy relationships.

By their own admission, most of the unhappy people I've helped train tell me that they either didn't choose their system for living, or they discovered that they don't like the system they once believed in. They were greatly influenced by others who didn't have their best interests in mind. I encourage these people to first start by admitting there is a problem and committing to an "I will" attitude versus an "I will try" attitude about making changes in their priorities and any negative behavior that is limiting their chances of achieving success.

As we age we find ourselves in a constant state of uncertainty regarding the pace that we want for our lives. Sorting out the pleasures of a simple life from the doldrums of pure boredom may be a daily occurrence for you. If you have a good job, if you have a support system in place, if you have faith in yourself, and if you have a strong work ethic, then you have everything you need to make positive changes. Maybe you have simply driven yourself to a hectic and unhappy place because you are chasing the life that someone you know already has. Big mistake. You need to focus on your goals and ambitions and avoid being envious of friends', neighbors', and coworkers' lifestyles.

If you fit the profile from the checklist above, you may be allowing others to determine who you are and how you feel about yourself. You're living under the social influence. Sooner or later, there will be that day of reconciliation when you realize how short life really is, and instead of allowing other people, financial burdens, or your work control you, you'll want to simplify your pursuits to only include what *you* believe is most important.

Why not make that day sooner rather than later? Keep reading.

Chapter 2

Focus on the process— not the outcome

L et's start at the very beginning. Anytime you are charged with managing people, coaching a team, raising a child, or teaching a class, it is far more productive to focus on incremental steps than to dwell on the final outcome. That's not to say that you shouldn't have expectations of the desired outcome, it is simply a way to keep from becoming frustrated along the way. For instance, if a state championship is the goal, speak of it as a team once in a while, but focus primarily on what has to be done in order to win that title. In business there is a saying: Always manage by objective. That's a great strategy once an unambiguous goal is determined and communicated. The process is the accomplishment of individual objectives; the outcome is achieving the established goal. I find that business and sports are a lot alike in this respect.

In almost every scenario described above, you are only really in charge for a short while. Think about coaching as an example. Athletes will move on to the next coach and then to one after that. Your job as the manager or supervisor is to instill the proper work ethic, habits, and other key business traits. People get promoted or change jobs. Teaching is the same, parenting is the same, and even at work your direct reports won't work for you forever. Think back to school and the best teachers, coaches, or counselors you have had. Replicate the way they instilled a work ethic in you. They are your motivational role models as you begin your career.

What really motivated you in high school or college? Was it grades, win/loss records, or a natural competitive spirit? Were you driven to achieve these things thanks to your mentors pushing you to become better? My guess is that the people who you remember most fondly will be the mentors who encouraged you to make strides toward doing your personal best. It's the collective personal bests that when combined in a strategic fashion add up to great team achievements. Work is no different. Great companies are nothing more than great people doing their collective best work, day in and day out.

Okay, so you want to make more money and get promoted quickly. Your first thought is to use this job as a means to get to the next one and then one day you will be the boss. The only thing wrong with that is if you focus solely on the outcome and not the process, you will get frustrated quickly. Whereas you will discover that your work can have more meaning and you can actually learn to love the job you currently have if you find creative ways to be great at it. You have two choices: You can be bored, go through the motions, and do a satisfactory job, OR you can do your job better than anyone who has come before you. If you do it better than it's ever been done, you will have loved that job and will be ready for the next one.

If you focus on the outcome alone, your work will seem like endless hours of frustration with no end in sight. End goals should be set but not obsessed over on a daily basis. This is a difficult message to convey to the generation of workers that have been labeled the "Me generation." My generation has caused some of this impatience in our children by encouraging behaviors such as "just take care of you." In the workplace, the company comes before the individual, and as parents of a generation entering the workforce, we need to encourage that mentality.

Parenting and working full time are an overwhelming combination. Maybe you feel that you will be—need to be— the perfect working mother. Guess what? There isn't such a thing. What there is plenty of are very tired, very frustrated working women ready to collapse at the end of the day or snap at anyone who asks if they need some extra help— say your own mother maybe? Believe it or not, you are not the first young mother who thinks they can have it all. Be realistic and patient.

Dads today want more time to be part of their kids' lives, and that is very tough with travel, late hours, and work-from-home expectations in the evenings. Providing for your family has not gone out of style. It's an expectation that is commendable. If you can't make every soccer game, explain to your kids the essential role you play and how you provide. They will learn a work ethic from watching what you do and how hard you work. Your example will stay with them their entire life. Many before you have gone through this very same process.

Just give your personal best as you were taught early on. As an employee, manager, or parent, no one expects more than that of you. If your personal best isn't good enough for your employer then chances are the fit just isn't right for either of you. The process can begin again without starting from scratch.

Formal education will make you a living; self-education will make you a fortune.

Jim Rohn, American author and motivational speaker

○ ○ ○

Have you stayed in touch with a mentor or role model you really admired?

_____

_____

_____

_____

Who are the most positive and supportive people in your life today?

_____

_____

_____

_____

Besides money, what motivates you to do better each day?

_____

_____

_____

_____

Chapter 3

Truly believe in what *you* believe is true

A life that is dedicated to strong beliefs, commitments, values, and ethics will truly become a life worth living. How can you make your life truly meaningful if you support a cause only when convenient or when it fits into your schedule? People with strong beliefs seem to enjoy life and are well grounded. On the flip side, pretending to believe in almost everything and overcommitting to the cause du jour simply adds to the chaos you should be trying to avoid. Saying no to half-hearted beliefs is just as important as saying yes to your true beliefs. Limit your volunteer time, financial support, and emotional capacity to what truly matters most.

Here are a couple of tough questions I get asked on a regular basis: Should your political and cultural beliefs define your career? Can your faith dictate your work ethic and habits? I say "absolutely" to both! Many great leaders have made their beliefs well known. Some do so knowing full well that it will limit their customer base, yet they are guided by core principles. Social influences don't sway their beliefs.

Many great companies have well-documented statements that come right from the personal beliefs of the CEO. These are core values instilled deep within these leaders, ones they are proud to share.

These owners empower their staff. They allow employees to switch product lines, create new advertising, and make hiring decisions. What they don't tolerate is a variance to their core beliefs and operating principles. The most successful leaders with strong core values also communicate them very effectively.

Social media is a primary way that causes and brands are advertised these days. Everyone wants you to be a fan or a friend of their business or product. I would challenge you to really think about how much time you spend on this and its overall importance. If you're constantly immersed in following your friends' and celebrities' Facebook updates and tweets, it's hard to even remember what you believe is most important. In this case, it's time to just unplug and remember who you are, and live out of that center.

This "cause of the month club" may be more harmful than a simple distraction. If you find yourself jumping on each bandwagon that passes by, the purpose for doing this might also have to do with popularity, the need to be noticed, misguided values, or even boredom. The reputation of being chameleon-like in philosophy will soon follow. That shallowness will never truly define you, nor will it lead to success or happiness.

Who you let influence and define the person you are is of top priority. While parents, educators, true friends, mentors, and leaders in faith are rightfully influential, only you can define the person you need to be. Rely on your core values to define yourself at work and in your personal life, and hopefully good synergy will develop between them. Especially for young ladies, never let anyone define you based upon your looks, weight, failed relationships, and other superficial factors. Keeping core values and beliefs intact is a far better way to define who you are. Know exactly who you are, what makes you that way, and be very proud of that.

Finding a job where your core values match that of the company's is a goal worth striving for. Don't compromise any values that make you uncomfortable or ashamed of what you do for a living. Somehow you need to figure out early on what or who inspires you. It may be volunteer work, it may not be. It may be something totally different than your work, but it's out there—I'm certain of it.

☐ ☐ ☐

Are you able to articulate the core values you've already established?

_____

_____

_____

_____

Do you have trouble saying no to every good cause that presents itself?

_____

_____

_____

_____

Can you tell the difference between true core values and those that are merely helpful or good?

_____

_____

_____

_____

Chapter 4

Be accountable
to yourself first

At the end of the day, do you own the problems you
have, or do you blame others for your chaotic and
complicated life? It's time to be honest with yourself:
Have your work or financial setbacks been self-induced for the
most part? An all too common example of this is the use of
credit as opposed to spending real money that you have earned.
Credit is a term used to describe the use of other people's money
and in exchange, paying a huge fee for doing so. What stinks is
that you eventually have to pay it back. It's never free or without
consequences.

I will probably never understand why teens and Millennials
share so much on their social media sites. I don't see the upside
or gain from doing this. I see all sorts of risks. What about
you? Do your Twitter posts seem to come back and haunt
you? Retweeting is the newest form of gossip, but unlike the
standard rumor mill, we start the problems ourselves. A good
friend of mine recently equated the use of Twitter in this decade
to smoking pot in the '70s as it relates to overall productivity.

It can be just as mind-numbing for young people and the new crutch for those determined not to directly interact with society.

Those who lack discipline have a tendency to get trapped in holes that they can't dig out of. Managing a reputation will become very similar to managing money. It is a currency that translates into your eventual worth to employers. By the way, old people do check your Facebook page, credit scores, and resources in an effort to explore your behavior outside of work. Inappropriate pictures are the worst possible reputation killer.

Do you find yourself to somehow always be in the middle of problems at work that you didn't create? Are you adding to the problem? Or are you finding quick and simple ways to fix the problem without making a scene? This is where your credibility can be built or destroyed. Upon spotting a problem, create healthy boundaries between you and disruptive coworkers immediately.

If you are by nature a negative person, please be mindful of how that comes across to others. Eventually, people tend to distance themselves from those who show a constant negative opinion about others or the business. That's not to say that taking an opposing view is bad, but when you do oppose an idea, deliver it with that an alternative suggestion to make something better. If you develop a reputation for constantly spewing negative thoughts, you will soon run out of people with whom to share them.

Don't be that person in the office who stirs things up just for excitement. Savvy corporate managers look for the common denominator in staffing problems. They quickly learn who is the real instigator of office drama. Don't be that person who keeps your boss up at night worrying what might happen tomorrow. Don't be the girl with the tattoo on your chest who complains of coworkers staring at your cleavage. You really must stop that behavior because nothing good ever comes from instigating office drama. All this will do is make you and those around you miserable.

Are you an overly competitive person by nature? Today's new workers have been raised to compete. All through school it's one highly competitive activity—sports, music, choir—after the next. All of this can be healthy, and if taken in the right context it can be a good way to prepare for the workforce. However, remember that the competition in an office environment isn't with the person next to you, the department next to yours, or the division on the floor above you. No, the competition is with other companies, not within your own. Focus your competitive spirit in a way that helps your employer, not yourself. By doing that, your credibility increases right along with your potential for advancement.

Brilliance is often undermined by bad behavior. Every organization has the man or woman we refer to as the BBHP. That stands for bad behavior/high performer. Those people wear you out. They meet the goals and objectives of the job, but in the process they wreak havoc within and demotivate the organization. These people are a manager's biggest headache because they have a very hard time justifying firing them, yet they have so much trouble managing the negative behavior that influences others. Look around your company, and if morale is low, my guess is a BBHP is in your midst. Please make sure that if morale is low in your company that it isn't because of you. It may stem from a misguided attempt at becoming influential.

I highly suggest taking an introspective look at yourself and how you have been influenced by others, and then envision how you would like to be influential one day. If you follow the right people when you are young, as you age and mature, the right people will then follow you. Here is an exceptional way to utilize a social platform in a positive fashion: Instead of being a person known to spread harmful stories and messages, become a person who can influence others in a positive way using lessons learned from your mentors.

Here's the bottom line: We develop habits either good or bad. Our habits are formed by our interests, our complications, insecurities, work ethic, and even addictions. Eventually, our habits define us and tell others all they need to know about who we are. Allow your habits to tell people about a great person.

☐ ☐ ☐

Is reputation management a priority and/or a concern for you?

_____

_____

_____

_____

Do you find yourself already caught up in too many workplace conflicts?

_____

_____

_____

_____

Who do you generally blame for your problems?

_____

_____

_____

_____

Chapter 5

Live on purpose

Hopefully you have a good sense of character and can identify others of great character. A person of great character can be the best role model for helping you shape your life. So what do you want to be, or be like? It's never too early to commit to a purpose or start writing a personal mission statement. A good beginning for this would be to think about and reduce to writing your most important values and how they capture your character and form the basis of your purpose in life. Try to have an honest answer ready if someone asks you what your goals, ambitions, and vision for your future looks like.

Generally speaking, I believe that it is possible to balance a hectic work schedule while maintaining healthy relationships. We tend to compromise the importance of our faith, family, and friends as we launch our careers, and we let these priorities slip. But one way technology has been extremely helpful is in helping us stay connected to others as we travel and work long hours. We should all carve out time each week to invest in our real relationships, regardless of where we are or what we're doing.

How early you start managing your time to build a balanced life will determine your outlook as a young professional. No matter how exceptional an employee you are today, over time true success (which is more than money and status) will eventually be measured differently.

Friendships can be restored later in life, I suppose, but life is very unpredictable. I actually feel sorry for young people who minimize the importance of their faith as bad things happen, like the loss of a family member. A strong faith allows us to cope with these situations as they arise and be far better equipped to provide comfort and support to others. Family involvement can be a great indicator of your future purpose-driven life regardless of the situation and relationship with your family or extend family. You can make a bad situation better and you can build upon a good situation to use as a model for your own family. You can learn from either situation. You use a good family situation as the model to strive for. You use a bad family situation as a clear path to avoid as you start your own family. Either way builds strong character. Avoidance is a sign of a weak character.

I'm of the opinion that all the career websites and social media job postings compound the problem the Millennial workforce has in putting down roots. Once you find the right job, unsubscribe from these sites to minimize the distractions. Millennials don't see job-hopping as a problem until they hear from a Human Resources manager that their work history has raised a red flag. Job-hopping may be the new norm, but the stability of being in one place will help you build a stronger sense of purpose.

Do you have a tendency to dream big and then do nothing about pursuing your big dream? This paves the path that leads to nowhere. There needs to be a road map of sorts that directs us away from the path toward complication and destructive outcomes. Having a purpose and a plan will guide our thoughts, words, and deeds as we make these selections. Establishing your list of uncompromised values will serve as a filter for the important decisions that are ahead of you.

Who do you really trust? Do you trust anyone even more than you trust yourself to help guide your decisions? Regardless if it's a parent, grandparent, sibling, or friend, the importance of open communications with a trusted and decent human being will help you gauge whether or not your intended purpose is meaningful. How is this purpose measured? Is it a meaningful purpose? Once you figure out who is the real judge on determining this, the way you live your life will begin to take shape.

The important lesson here is to become grounded and build a solid foundation as early as you can. Get established from the outset as a person of integrity, honesty, and a strong work ethic. This will develop sharp instincts so you can quickly become someone that just knows what to do and then does it.

You can forgive a person for bad decisions or poor execution, but you can't forgive them for a lack of character.

Peter Drucker, author and business expert

○ ○ ○

How well would you say you are doing with having a balanced lifestyle?

_____

_____

_____

_____

Are you setting attainable goals and working toward them yet?

_____

_____

_____

_____

Are you willing to be a mentor or be mentored?

_____

_____

_____

_____

Chapter 6

Carve out decision-making time every day

I f you have a hectic life, I strongly suggest that you carve out a small part of your day when you make the most important decisions. You don't have to be alone, but you should be alone with your friends or family in a quiet, relaxing setting that removes you from the stress of the day. Maybe before the kids wake up, or after they go to bed, you can find time to reflect on what is truly important and what really is the most meaningful to you.

This quiet-time concept might seem next to impossible, but the outcome produces better decisions and then will free you up to properly enjoy doing the things you like or that need 100 percent of your attention to get done. When are you at your best during the day? Some people exercise in the morning because they find this "me" time helps them to arrive at better decisions than when they are forced to make a hasty conclusion in the heat of battle. I highly suggest that you defer any high-level decisions until you are in the most effective and "best" part of your day. This concept also supports the twenty-four-hour rule where emotionally charged decisions should be held off until ample time has passed for your response. You will be amazed how much your position can change in just one day. The timing of when you reach key decision points is a fundamental foundation builder for future success.

Our current pace has made it very hard to relax, and it seems as if we are taking care of everyone but ourselves. When overly stressed, it's pretty common to make spur of the moment decisions based on emotion rather than core business principles or taking every aspect of the decision into account. Over time you will become more aware of when and where you make the best decisions.

You need to take good care of yourself first. Those of you who are inherently "people-pleasers" know exactly what this means. People pleasing is going to burn you out fast unless you find a little time each day for yourself. When major decisions need to be made and you are not at your best, it's not a bad idea to involve others who are affected and examine every angle of the situation. There will be times that you will need to slow down to get ahead.

I applaud the Millennials who have a healthy respect for the quality of life and balance of work and family. When we are young we tend to undervalue the quality of life, believing there will always be more time once we make it. An example of this is quitting a job you love for one that you will hate, but it pays more money. Money is important for sure, but not at the expense of everything else. Recently, I've heard many stories of young business professionals passing up significant pay increases to stay with a job and company they love. I commend our new workforce for that type of quality-of-life decision making.

At work you can find that unique thing that makes your workday special and allows your personal brand to become part of the organization. It could be striving for excellence in every task. It might be as simple as saying good morning to each coworker. It might be asking if anyone needs your help on a regular basis. Regardless how simple or subtle, it can build your reputation, establish a personal brand, and help you achieve a better quality of life for yourself and others.

The best part of your day can be when you have had an opportunity to make others feel better or special too. If you have that people-pleaser mentality, you already are being rewarded by the positive feelings from helping others get to a better place. Your self-satisfaction may be driven by the kindness and caring you give to others. At least take a few seconds to pause and reflect on the importance of helping others to validate the importance of your time. If you do this well and continue to build upon this, you will live a pretty darn good life.

The quality of a person's life is in direct proportion to their commitment to excellence, regardless of their chosen field or endeavor.

Vince Lombardi, legendary football coach

○ ○ ○

Have you made too many decisions in the heat of the moment? How can you correct that?

_____

_____

_____

Can you set aside ten minutes each day to make important decisions?

_____

_____

_____

_____

PART 2

THE SOCIAL
INFLUENCE @ WORK

Chapter 7

Work at work

So, you have your first "real" job now. How is it going? Do you wake up dreading having to go to work? Guess why they call it work? Because it *is* work and it's not always fun. You don't go to "fun" every day, or that's not why you get paid anyway. You have to work for your money and lifestyle. Not every hour is Happy Hour in most workplaces. Here's the deal—you are there to improve the profitability of the company. Sure, you can—and should— have fun at work. Some of the best and most profitable companies encourage fun and have activities geared toward that. But remember, it is work, and for that you receive a paycheck. You should consider it a privilege every day and every week you earn a paycheck. Ask yourself: Did I give my employer more value today than what she paid me? Did I generate revenue for my employer, save her money, or improve customer relations? Or did I play games, update my Facebook page, and download YouTube videos, wasting my time and my employer's money?

Human Resources managers, senior directors, and business owners all look for what value you can bring to the organization. Likewise, you should have that same mindset and be prepared to address it as early as the interview process. In many cases, the hiring decision is based upon which candidate demonstrates that the best, and the same goes for promotions. For example, an employer may be looking for someone who can be a mature and calming influence in a stressful position, or he could be looking for someone who can bring a higher level of energy to a department that has become known as a mundane and boring place. Having a keen sense of awareness about the value you can bring is a key element in becoming a highly desirable employee.

Give more than the job description requires of you. Sure, you need to focus primarily on the task at hand and get that work done, but I don't know any business owner who has fired someone for giving extra. Giving just a little extra effort during idle times, instead of socializing or surfing the web, could make a huge difference in your career. The famous American inventor Thomas Edison once said, "Opportunity is missed by most people because it is dressed in overalls and looks like work."

A great way for tech-savvy employees to be productive and provide value is to make good use of social media skills by offering their expertise to build a strong brand awareness presence or even do some social selling and marketing in relevant areas. Use your crowd-sourcing expertise to the benefit of your company. While many bosses won't get this at first, when they see the results of your work or the increased revenue produced, they will catch on quickly. I've seen where offering up these ideas and talents can be a pathway to advancement. It sure beats hiding out and pretending to be busy.

Time is money. If you provide your organization less value than what you earn, you are stealing from your employer. A positive attitude and good behavior—not complaining, not posturing, not threatening to leave—will drive you as high in the organization as you want to go. Don't ever buy into the idea that you are indispensable, or that you can quit today and find a better job tomorrow. Everyone, including you, can be replaced.

Before you ever threaten to quit and start your own business, remember this: There is a big difference between having what is required to run a successful business and a strong work ethic, job skills, and knowledge. The key to being a successful business owner is the combination of all these things and having the appetite for risk. Most start-ups fail. They do so because the new venture wasn't properly funded, and the new owner wasn't willing to risk it all to make it successful. You may well be smarter than the owner of your company, but don't ever underestimate the amount of risk he or she took to launch the business.

There are a lot of things that go into creating success. I don't like to do just the things I like to do. I like to do things that cause the company to succeed. I don't spend a lot of time doing my favorite activities.

Michael Dell

◯ ◯ ◯

Do you have a good sense of what you can be doing during idle times that is productive?

_____

_____

_____

_____

Do you feel productive and valuable to your employer every day?

_____

_____

_____

_____

Chapter 8

Avoid the "progressive workplace" trap

Sure, everybody wants to work for Google. But you know what? Those people work hard, and they work long hours. One day the shareholders will influence the perks and start trimming nonessential costs and looking for savings. All companies go through a lifecycle like this, and then they get down to basic business principles.

Savvy Millennial employers create an illusion of posting jobs that don't look or feel like work. Their recruiting webpages are filled with fun-loving photos and graphics. They show images of employees updating their Facebook pages and tweeting throughout the day. They are creating these images and workplace party scenarios primarily for the purpose of offering jobs that pay less than their competitors. It is not always as it seems, unless the leadership of the organization truly believes in that culture. Be careful not to go into a job at a trendy workplace expecting that the job isn't really hard work or long hours. Don't believe for a minute that because you can wear shorts to work that performance is not required or that they have an anything-goes employment policy. That seldom happens in the real world. You can get fired for performance issues there as easily as anywhere else. Business is business.

It's been reported in a 2012 intergenerational work survey that 33 percent of young professionals would take a pay cut in order to have unlimited access to social media during the workday. The study suggests that freedom to use their social platforms during the day is a top priority for these young workers. To me, this sends a signal that an employee is confusing work time with playtime and may have some serious issues over being disconnected from his social life for more than a few hours. Mobility has compounded the problem and further blurred the line between work and social time frames. Gaming via mobile devices has become a major distraction for young professionals. The temptation for avid gamers to engage in this activity during the workday is increasing. This is a workplace trap and a great way to get fired. Yes, you can and will get fired if you are caught playing games during work hours.

In recent years, with the down economy, young professionals have become somewhat fearful of being fired—so much so they almost hideout in the workplace, staying below the radar. This generation has witnessed family members being downsized from their jobs and watched the emotional strain caused when they struggle to find employment at the rate of pay they once had. They think that by becoming invisible or by never taking risks, they can stay safe and not be fired. Please know that good bosses don't shoot the messenger.

Here is the right way to become "fire-proof": Figure out how to become indispensable to your boss and employer. This is one of the hardest lessons in life, but the key is to figure this out before you get fired, rather than learning from mistakes made. Being fire-proof isn't just one thing, but rather a combination of everything that you believe applied to your work. The core values instilled in you earlier in life, your education, and the knowledge of your job all combine to make you an exceptional asset to your employer. Whether you produce or support, you need to constantly demonstrate your worth to the company by providing value to your employer well beyond what you cost on the payroll. The hardest part of all is that this must happen every day, not just most days.

Progressive workplaces often attract seemingly invincible employees. These self-confident, highly-motivated game changers might rush in to evoke radical change, establish record performance, get promoted, and then in a few short years become company president. On the other hand, the boss might get frustrated with the self-confident game changer's lack of appreciation of the company's current style and attitude toward doing the heavy lifting, and the aggressive employee might find she isn't quite as invincible as she thought. It's quite important to be realistic about being indispensable and invincible. It's equally important to know that having this mindset can leave you with unrealistic expectations of your job security.

I prefer employees who are filled with humility and have a self-effacing style of leadership. They seem to appreciate the job they do have and stay focused on that until ready for the next challenge. The most valued employees seem to adapt quickly to the company's culture, regardless of the progressive or traditional culture. The great employees know how they can be indispensable, but they will never consider themselves to be irreplaceable.

○ ○ ○

How would you rank your value to the organization thus far?

_____

_____

_____

_____

How important is job security to you?

_____

_____

_____

_____

Chapter 9

Keep tattoos and piercings in hidden places only

The advice that I would give any young person (let's pretend they would ask) is to act and look as your future spouse and/or future boss might desire. Here's the deal—when you select your body art, you may do so as an expression of your beliefs, a symbol of freedom, or even a tribute to a special person or family member. I get that. But when a Human Resources director sees your act of self-expression, they don't exactly see it the same way you do. Instead they form a lasting first impression. They might see you as someone who has made some bad decisions and wonder how many more bad decisions you will make if they hire you. So you had better be careful and smart and have a twenty-four-hour rule in place when making your decision on this.

When interviewing for a new job, you have to dress up. Hopefully you can cover up any body art and look as professional as you can to make that first impression. Make sure you do your homework on company culture before showing up for your interview, but avoid dressing like your Facebook friend who already works there and told you it would be cool to just wear jeans. Dress up!

A Human Resources consultant who advises corporate hiring managers on best practices recently told me that they are seeing more and more where the expressive forms of body art are limiting career-changing opportunities. It's now at the same criteria level as a person's education. In other words, they are seeing a rise in the number young people being passed over, merely based upon appearance, in favor of other applicants with similar credentials. If two applicants for the same position were in front of a hiring manager, they will pick the person whose appearance matches the company image best.

The attitude toward ruling out someone because of visible tattoos may ease off some as more young people get tattoos. Certainly the more creative companies and those operating remotely from their customers have little reluctance to hire based upon this. Currently, 40 percent of twenty-six to forty-year-olds have at least one tattoo, according to a Pew Research study. Not surprising to me is that the laser tattoo removal business is booming, showing an annual increase of 32 percent in 2011 alone, according to a study by *The Patient's Guide*. The number one reason cited for removal? Employment reasons.

To a hiring manager, your body art is not an indication of a free spirit or a risk-taker but simply an example of showing poor judgment. Employers look at past performance and behavior as the leading indicator of future behavior. Think carefully on this: It isn't about a middle-age businessman who wears a suit and tie every day expecting you to look like him; no, this is about past decisions you've made being an indication of the future decisions you will make.

The bottom line is this: What seems cool and hip at twenty-one might end up limiting your opportunities down the road. I personally don't care nor do I judge others regarding this, but I sure know plenty of business owners who do, have, and always will. If you are going to express yourself with body art of some sort, make it so that it can be hidden during a job interview. Likewise, think about what a permanent marking might look like when you are fifty or older. I would guess that very few middle- age people are actually pleased with a tattoo from years past.

Appearance is a crucial hiring decision in businesses where first impressions really matter. It just is. This subject goes far beyond the obvious. It's the professional hairstyle, the clean and well-groomed look, the body language, and the attitude. What's important to a business owner or manager is the image of their company, not just sales or service. In order to sustain a healthy company, a business owner will carefully select employees who build upon, not try to change, the culture of the business they have created. If an employer's business requires working with the public or demonstrating trust, think how your appearance can add to, not take away from, that situation.

One company I visited shared its policy for employees attending picnics and golf outings, citing that no visible body art or suggestive clothing would be tolerated at these events. Several employees had to forgo these social outings. If your company has a casual day, please dress like you're going to work, not the beach. Use good judgment, even when dressing down is allowed.

So do what you want—but you'd better be right. In the end what really matters isn't your good looks or trendy hairstyles. What matters is the way you present yourself in the workplace and the responsibility you take to show your company that its image will always take priority over your need for self-expression. Your appearance should project a positive and professional image, be neat and clean, and be completely in sync with your company's promise to the customer. This, combined with a positive attitude and cheerful smile, is a giant step toward success.

○ ○ ○

Are you willing to put the best interests of the company before your need for self-expression?

_____
_____
_____
_____

Do you look and feel the part in fitting within the company culture and image?

_____
_____
_____
_____

Chapter 10

Don't be stupid

One stupid tweet can unravel a career. One night, while having drinks with coworkers, a young woman in our industry posted on Twitter, "My boss just left; now we can talk about him." A former coworker retweeted and added, "Hopefully he left before creeping everyone out." Dozens more tweets followed and eventually the whole company read what was out there. It was a matter of days before the termination occurred.

A young man in our industry had a strong reputation as one of the best and brightest upcoming employees in his company. The company Facebook page boasted of his accomplishments, credentials, and industry certifications. As this company was competing for a major project, his name was given to the client as the lead project manager if they were to be awarded the project. The client, wanting to ensure that the "moral fiber" of the young project manager was consistent with the environment they established for their own employees, began searching his social media presence. In a matter of hours, our member company received the following two-sentence e-mail: "Upon our review of the proposals and due diligence completed, we have selected a different firm to perform this work. The primary factor in our decision was the inconsistency in our core values to that of the assigned project manager as witnessed on his personal Facebook page." That is social stupidity.

Your Facebook page can be filled with closet skeletons. Don't be surprised to have an employer, or prospective employer, ask to have you unlock the privacy and security controls on the spot so they can see what only your friends see. If done wrong, your timeline can be a nightmare of embarrassing moments that you will need to explain. Creating a public page and a private page under an alias is another bad idea. Sure, it hides the party scenes from your employer, but it robs you of precious time you can be spending on important things. Managing two Facebook accounts is a pretty clear indication that you are under the social influence.

Your friend list is public information on Facebook. If an employer asks to be your "friend," it's often to see the type of people you hang out with. Clean this up before allowing this to happen. If you are concerned about privacy, then the Internet isn't a great place to post pictures of you doing something stupid.

It's a huge mistake to assume that your work superiors won't see your on-line social presence—they will. Your lifestyle is their business. Company leaders that value the core belief in living a wholesome lifestyle will only embrace those whose "total life" is consistent with theirs. Please know that what you put out there is for everyone to see. A good rule to follow is to not post anything you wouldn't want your grandmother or pastor to see.

Social mistakes also happen when you try to show your importance. A well-known keynote speaker I heard recently described how a major US corporation recruits and hires new college graduates. Their core principles revolved around ethics, humility, fairness to others, and gratitude. This company flew every prospect into their corporate headquarters and picked them up at the airport. Unknowingly, the interview began at baggage claim. The driver was a company employee from the HR department, not an independent limo driver as it may have seemed. Every good or bad behavior was noted. Each conversation, polite or rude comments, agitated or gracious remarks, belittling or appreciative language, was documented and ranked. You see, this was the first test and often the only real test for some candidates in finding the right cultural fit for their business. About half of the candidates were never really considered by the time they arrived at the company's offices.

This company was recruiting the best and brightest. They were doing this to screen new hires that came in with an attitude of self-importance and entitlement. They only wanted people with an inherent attitude of human kindness and respect. Prior to doing this, they were spending around $9,000 per bad hire. Following this new process, the attrition rate in the first year went from 20 percent to nearly zero. There is so much to learn from these stories.

In the 2012 Summer Olympics, two athletes were dismissed from their teams for sending inappropriate tweets. This cost them the opportunity to represent their country on a far more important platform than what the tweet could have ever gained them. It's an example of wanting to feel more important than their peers, but in the end choosing a common delivery method that made them no different from anyone else. They were living under the social influence and being foolishly courageous. "Followers" and "likes" become addictive and build a false sense of self-importance that can lead to a misplaced sense of courage when you post something. My generation doesn't see spewing private matters, spreading rumors, or sharing favorite song lyrics via digital mass media as anything but reckless.

Don't tweet or text while drinking. Drunk-dialing is bad enough, and the worst is an incoherent voicemail the next day. Under-the-influence messaging is a stupid idea, and it can lead to some lasting repercussions. Think about why you would say something to the world that seems funny or important—and do it the next day if it still seems relevant. Everything you send electronically is out there for everyone to see, and trusting friends not to retweet is just being stupid. Most of the time it's just TMI (too much information) and your not-so-close friends from several years ago will pass it along just to make you look silly. If you are addicted to achieving more and more friend requests, likes, retweets, etc., then you need to find something besides social media to build your self-esteem.

These are extremely important lessons and examples of bad behavior. If you take a realistic look at yourself and the baggage you may have, how would you stack up against a room of potential new hires with the same relative education and skill sets? This is where you have to be smarter than the pack. Rarely do hiring managers compare grade point averages unless every applicant attended the same college or university. What they are more likely to compare are tendencies employees and potential new hires have to do things either helpful or harmful to the company's reputation.

Social platforms have made your personal life exposed for all to see. Before the transparency of the Internet, a barrier was established between work life and social life. Today if you make the decision to be active on social platforms, you give up the right to keep your personal affairs separate from what your employer knows about you. As much as we would like to have our personal life not have a negative impact on our career, those days are gone.

○ ○ ○

Do you keep a healthy separation between social platforms at work and personal networking?

_____

_____

_____

_____

Is your career more important than being perceived as hip and cool on your social sites?

_____

_____

_____

_____

Does your company have a policy for using social media, and do you understand it and follow it?

_____

_____

_____

_____

Chapter 11

Save the drama

It's very important to know the difference between being dramatic and being interesting. Too many young people don't understand the difference. Likewise, repeating something interesting you heard or read on the Internet, as opposed to sharing your unique and interesting thoughts, are very different. I'm of the opinion that workplace drama starts when coworkers run out of interesting things to discuss. Drama in the workplace is something that wears out quickly and limits the potential of many creative individuals. Generally this stems from pure boredom or lack of ongoing challenges. I'm convinced the leading cause of Millennial workplace boredom stems from overstimulation as a child with too many activities and sensory stimulants.

Too much drama also occurs when aggressive or upwardly mobile individuals have the misguided belief that the attention drama brings will somehow make an employee more important. Remember, this isn't high school! It's not your summer job where gossip, tweeting, smoking dope out back, gaming, wasting time, or degrading others was acceptable behavior. To keep a good job you need to quickly transition from being socially reckless to responsible in every facet of your life.

At home, family drama is very common and most often equally as unnecessary. This too should be replaced with conversation, care, and compassion. "Carryover" drama (an unfulfilled need for attention) is the result of having a bad day at work. But why should your spouse get punished for that? Likewise, it could be your coworkers who pay the price for you having a spat with the spouse the night before. This needs to be checked at the door in both scenarios. The ability to separate the drama in your work life from your life at home is a crucial balancing act that needs constant monitoring. The best employees have the ability to push through problems at home, promptly deal with the situation after hours, and not let it negatively affect their job.

Please set healthy boundaries. It's okay to be a complicated person as long as that is appreciated by those who have to bear the brunt of your quirkiness and mood changes. Being unnecessarily complicated can make you miserable, and of course do the same for those around you. Setting rational boundaries for these self-inflicted complications is a must for the workplace. Dragging a complicated personal life into work is an awful idea.

Like every entrepreneur, I've had my share of bad days at work. One of my worst days was about twenty years ago when a highly valued female employee decided to offer a friendly suggestion to another highly valued female employee on how she should be raising her children. It started innocently enough over a concern about a friend of one of the lady's children. What started out as a "thought you should know" ended in a shouting match. No matter what intervention our management team attempted, these ladies never willingly spoke to one another again. Within months, they both left the company over this unfortunate incident. An office friendship, without the presence of a healthy boundary, dissolved within minutes over a very sensitive personal matter, and the company had to find, train, and rebuild most of a department. What was said was said, and no one could unring that bell.

Make every attempt not to communicate via e-mail, as it is a very impersonal method. E-mail is an excellent tool for documenting previous conversations, events, meetings, or making announcements. E-mail is a horrible choice for explaining an emotional feeling or sharing private thoughts. A couple of things to remember: One, don't send anything via e-mail you wouldn't want printed in the local newspaper, and two, when you use caps, highlights, italics, or any other fonts or punctuation, others may not understand your emphasis. The bottom line is that human interaction is still the best place to share emotions, even if it makes you uncomfortable.

Put yourself in a management position where you need to decide about the promotion of two equally qualified employees: one a drama queen, the other a heads-down, nonconfrontational, focused, and productive team player who avoids office rumors and scandals. Which one gets the promotion? It's pretty simple to see this when you're the boss; not so easy when you are caught up in the drama. Your credibility and reputation, either good or bad, follows you for a long, long time. Word of mouth spreads fast, but worse yet, word of "mouse" spreads exponentially faster.

Excessive drama creates unhappy people. Unhappy people in the workplace often get that way because others begin to avoid them. It's compounded when coworkers quit listening to their ideas that have turned negative. When the drama fails to gain attention, unhappy people turn to negative behaviors. As one of my favorite business advisers puts it, the way to improve employee happiness is to fire all the unhappy people.

◯ ◯ ◯

Are you a stabilizing or disruptive force in your organization?

_____

_____

_____

_____

What form of restraint do you maintain for the effective use of e-mail?

_____

_____

_____

_____

Do you see yourself as a morale builder, or do you deflate morale?

_____

_____

_____

_____

Chapter 12

Build workplace trust

Every dysfunctional relationship you will ever encounter at work will be the result of poor communication or a lack of trust. Likewise, rebuilding trust will be the foundation for working toward repairing any bad relationship. This is true with family, friends, coworkers, or any others in your life. The foundation of any solid relationship begins with trusting others to make good decisions. Today's society (and our parents) have taught us not to trust strangers and, in many circumstances, rightfully so. However, somewhere along the line we have to trust those around us to make decisions on our behalf. I bet you trust almost every friend and family member. Likewise, you will eventually learn to trust the leaders in your company. I think we need to give our coworkers the benefit of the doubt, and let them prove we can't trust them instead of thinking we can't from the start. This is a very counterintuitive premise in today's society.

Trust is a funny thing, most often based on an instinct or trait predetermined well before one enters the workplace. A lack of trust in authority figures often leads to a bad working relationship with your boss. The premise of trust in the workplace is based on the overall organizational structure of a company. The lack of communication is simply ironic when you consider we live in a world of major technological advancements and with every tool imaginable for improving communication.

It is very common in the workplace for employees to never get to a place of trust with their superiors. This results in constant challenging of authority and a perceived unwillingness to be led. Nothing frustrates an employer as much as having their employees constantly question their decisions. On the other hand, once trust is established, viewing decisions with a critical eye is why key employees are valued so much. So, the fine line is knowing when you have earned the right to question workplace authority. It's best to wait until you have entered that inner circle that has this level of trust well established.

A very common source of conflict begins with employees showing disrespect for company leaders. This is one of the most difficult concepts of all for young employees to grasp as the questioning of authority has become a widely accepted trend in politics, religion, and in family institutions. It's very hard for a company to define its expectations on showing respect for one another, demanding obedience, controlling defiance, and resolution of conflict. Likewise, it's very difficult to put into the employee handbook how to resolve conflict beyond just describing a process. When to apply assertiveness and when to offer up cooperation in emotionally clouded situations ultimately depends upon the level of respect for the other person. Just like in a family situation, workplace conflicts resulting from a lack of respect can lead to some very hurt feelings and repairing them can be nearly impossible.

Authority does have limits, and by closely monitoring your core values, principles, and ethics, along with knowing company policy and procedure, authority can be managed. You have the tools to respect authority but not allow a person in an authority role to abuse them or you. Standing up to this is tough and is often seen as defiance. Yet if you know what is right, what the policy is, and what your instincts tell you, it is appropriate to persuade, appeal, and try to change the course of the authority figure to do the right thing.

You might find yourself just having a bad boss whose values, principles, and ethics simply do not match yours. I'll always remember a visit to a leading company in our industry back in the late '90s. This troubled firm was struggling with managerial problems. They boasted the traditional motto of the customer being right and had empowered employees to always error on the side of the client. I was asked to evaluate the excessive turnover, and to offer a recommendation on how to correct it. Almost immediately, you could see a huge disconnect between philosophy and reality. I quickly discovered this company (it's no longer in business) never once practiced the slogan they marketed. Every employee at every level knew this was true and made it a standing joke. The credibility from the top down was shot. There was no respect or trust for leadership. They had a bad boss, not a turnover problem, and as it turned out, many of the employees who bailed out are now very successful in new companies. In these situations the right thing to do is quit. Don't compromise your core values to fit into an organization of questionable ethics.

One of the best definitions of workplace trust I can share is this: "Trust is making and meeting commitments without follow up." From my experience, unless you are in a family-owned business workplace, trust doesn't necessarily have to be based upon an in-depth personal relationship. It's more about business, getting the job done, and not letting others down who depend on you.

If you are in a position of trust with company finances, always treat this with the utmost respect and care. Treat your employer's money even more carefully than you would your own. Understand and obey each policy governing travel, expenses, reimbursements, and supplies. Never ever let the temptation of taking more than what is earned erode the trust you've earned. From day one, be known as an employee with high-ethical standards and a person who everyone can trust.

As you gain experience you will earn the trust of management. This is a process, and it must first start with asking permission on a new idea or initiative, then it moves to simply expressing intent to move forward, and then one day you move forward and just report on the progress. Keep in mind you have to follow all the steps until trust has been earned. Jumping the gun on this will break down the trust you are trying to build.

It is possible to rebuild lost trust in personal and professional business relationships, but it is difficult. It takes time and direct confrontation. The issues of lost trust simply have to be stripped down to the essence of the problem. Often, we lose trust as a result of a problem we couldn't directly confront someone about, or we have chosen through fear of conflict to triangulate and involve a party that is more approachable. The avoidance of a direct conversation in lieu of several easier non-direct discussions to vent frustration or concern is a direct pathway to eroding a relationship. For example, if you find yourself having to be at a party in order to find out what your friends or coworkers are up to, then a red flag should be waving. There is a communication problem that needs attention. Having enough trust in a relationship to address any type of problem is a relationship worth having and fighting to maintain.

○ ○ ○

Do you have a tendency to hold a grudge after conflict?

_____

_____

_____

_____

Can you see yourself trusting someone enough to be your mentor?

_____

_____

_____

_____

Chapter 13

Learn to fit in
to company culture

Working for an entrepreneur is very different from working for a large corporation as it relates to fitting into the culture of the business. It's crucial that you understand the importance of the culture and how vastly different it can be from one business to the next. You need to fit into that culture and adapt to it as quickly as possible to succeed. Every company has a unique culture and makes changes at its own pace. It's important you learn both very quickly.

Large corporations (with the exception of the Millennial-friendly tech firms) generally have a more structured and rigid business philosophy driven from the top down under the watchful eye of a board of directors that has established a set or core principles. This, combined with shareholder expectations, drives business decisions and hiring practices. In companies large or small you can get ahead so much faster if you think like the owner instead of a clock puncher.

Entrepreneurial companies generally have a culture reflecting the founder and owner's core values. That owner will try desperately to build his or her company without changing these core principles or compromising the vision he or she originally had for the firm. It is essential to quickly learn what the owner is most passionate about with staffing. It may be a self-effacing humility in the employees—to show kindness and empathy and care for their customers. It could be the complete opposite, looking more for the hard-charging, untiring workaholics that will squeeze every penny from a customer.

Following a motivational speech I gave to a group of college graduates, I asked if any of them had a question about the many choices and great opportunities in front of them. A young man stood up and said, "My instructors told me there is a high demand for my skills. Does this mean that I won't get fired for not showing up or being late on occasion?" I explained to him and his classmates that strong ambition and high-energy levels are much better traits to have, and that they will work in every size and type of job. There is no better way to get hired and stay employed than to have a serious commitment to giving 100 percent every day. I've found that employees who have good and bad days usually end up having more bad ones than good ones as the job becomes routine. These people take themselves out of consideration for advancement because of their behavior in their current position. Being passed over for promotion starts a cycle of boredom that leads to them becoming job-hoppers.

I've studied and coached a lot of healthy and dysfunctional companies and their respective management teams. What I've concluded is that regardless of size, the two biggest obstacles in a dysfunctional organization are the overinflated male ego and the hypersensitivity of some women. Wow! A bold statement for sure, yet look around you, listen to workplace conversations, and study the human behavior and body language of your coworkers. Can you spot this behavior and distance yourself from it? People posture in order to get the things they want, especially in a workplace where a lack of communication fuels uncertainty.

Office politics, as it's sometimes called, is a by-product of posturing that seems necessary to accomplish short-term results. More times than not, the instigators of office politics have no real plan in place. They haven't developed their end game beyond the next promotion, the next week, or the next month. Office politics is very unnecessary and typically a sign of boredom. As an employee caught up in office politics, end it quickly. When you become known for being involved in these situations, I guarantee your boss is starting to question your productivity. Think about it; then dial it back if you fall into this category.

My guess is that you haven't been hired to be the company whistle-blower or to point out the flaws of your coworkers. One great piece of advice I received early in my career: Always praise others publicly and complain about or criticize others privately. Even in obvious situations, keep anything negative to as few people as absolutely necessary and let your immediate supervisor determine where it goes from there.

The workplace can feel like a battlefield if an overly confrontational environment is encouraged or tolerated. Don't get sucked into this. Values, morals, policy, procedures, and your supervisor's directives should determine the battles you choose to fight. Popularity, importance, building self-esteem, turf protection, and a propensity for argumentative behavior shouldn't determine your battles. The worst battles are the ones that find everyone in the boss's office with the door shut, asking him or her for immediate clarification and/or to choose a side.

If this seems to happen to you a lot, stop it. Stop it before you become known as a disruptive employee. Stop it before you become labeled as high maintenance. If your boss continuously has to mediate your decision making or keeps getting drawn into your battles, then he is not doing his or her job effectively. You have been hired to add value, not take away from the value someone else is providing. Stop it, and learn to let it go.

Difficult situations occur in every workplace. Organizations whose culture is driven from the top and effectively communicated to all seem to rate very high with young employees, and are typically very good at handling challenging problems as they arise. It works that way because the focus is on the common goals, the work itself, and the results.

I was visiting a company this past year, and the owner shared a few stories about his young workforce. He encouraged open communication, and he welcomed suggestions from everyone. He shared with me that he was growing discouraged and was considering changing this policy, as his bright new employees just didn't mesh well with the older employees. As we examined the situation, we found that generational battle lines had been drawn in his company and each side (somewhere around age forty) had been trying to expose the other group's weaknesses rather than work together. The suggestions had all deteriorated into complaints. One of my favorite suggestions came from an older employee who wrote, "We would be doing much better if we blocked the Internet access, as the new kids in marketing play a computer game called LinkedIn all day." I found that misconception quite amusing.

The open communication had become mudslinging between the two generations. His office was the frontline each time a confrontation boiled over. On one occasion, the company's young IT manager decided to switch to a new web-based software package in a department made up of primarily older employees. As it was discovered later, his motivation wasn't to improve efficiencies or save money, it was to expose the older employees' technological weaknesses and to prove his point about their reluctance to learn new skills. He did make a pretty good point, but he lost his job in the process.

What we discovered was simple: Over time, this entrepreneur had forgotten to share with his employees what made his company great in the first place. He was assuming that middle management was conveying those core operating philosophies with new hires. Instead they became threatened by the youth movement and used their positions of authority to minimize the technological benefits the owner wanted from the new employees. It was an unfortunate mess that he never expected. The small business that he founded was being ruined by a growing political and generational divide. This owner had to set some employees free, and he has reappointed himself as the keeper of the company culture. His business is now back on track because everyone who remains understands the culture, acceptable behavior, team goals, and his definition of mutual respect.

○ ○ ○

Are you able to accept the established procedures of your company and excel at your job operating under them?

_____

_____

_____

_____

Have you avoided office politics or been sucked into them?

_____

_____

_____

_____

Are you able to tell if this organization is a good cultural fit for you long term?

_____

_____

_____

_____

Chapter 14

My new boss is a woman!

One of the most puzzling, complicated, and confusing business challenges for me to understand is why so many people have trouble working for women, especially women who report to other women. Why is this even a problem? Here's one theory I have: It starts from being peers. I've seen dozens of conflicts that begin when one manager is promoted to head a department of people with whom they were once business peers. In most cases, I find this to be a lack of respect or a lack of understanding of how the organizational structure of a company works and the importance of a chain of command. Ladies, deal with it.

And men, listen up. It's the twenty-first century. How can men still have a problem reporting to women? As a person of strong faith, I understand the biblical interpretations of authority and appreciate the traditional conflicts that the workplace could invoke. I also understand the old-school workplace traditions and how uncommon it used to be to report to a female. Traditional thinking and the attachment to outdated leadership methods simply must yield to hiring the best qualified candidate, regardless of gender. Needless to say, there is a change that has occurred in the last several decades where more women seek higher education and have sacrificed non-work priorities to climb the corporate ladder. It is my strong opinion that they should be given the exact same level of respect (and compensation) as a man in the workplace. Guys, deal with it.

Now, for the woman who is the new boss, here's what you need to deal with: The reality is that you need to manage your friendships differently now. Coworkers, who were your peers and friends, can remain your friends, but new boundaries have to be established. Especially when you're dealing with confidential information, draw a line and never, ever cross it. This is true for men who get promoted as well: things do and will change, and please don't become oversensitive to now being left out of after-work activities and social interaction. The deal is that because you are now in management, your old peers feel as if you left them and harbor some resentment. Likewise, you will feel resentment from being detached from them. It's just the natural way of things for both sides. Learn to deal with it.

The biggest mistake a young manager can make following their promotion is to demand respect in the early stages of their new position. A much better approach is to earn respect, and the way to do that is to stay true to your fundamental beliefs, such as your work ethic, integrity, honesty and general ethics. Just because you were promoted does not mean you should change anything about your core values and principles. What was the right thing to do before being promoted is still the right thing.

Sometimes we just have to work through the conflict. Often, the relationship between a newly promoted female manager and her staff evolves into a massive defiance disorder where every directive is suddenly challenged. The new manager needs to recognize what her former peers are feeling and going through. Those who felt passed over need to accept the reality and find ways to support their new boss. This all takes time and proper communication. This is where maturity from all parties involved will be tested. This is also a time where everyone needs to think carefully as they choose their words and write e-mails. Maturity, a gender-neutral behavior, will make or break this situation. Remember that showing maturity is a great way to be considered for the next promotion.

○ ○ ○

Does gender matter to you at work?

_____

_____

_____

_____

Do you find it easier to communicate better with men or women?

_____

_____

_____

_____

Chapter 15

Be fully aware
in every situation

I don't believe the Millennial workforce can be classified as selfish or lazy, but I do see room for improvement with their overall lack of perception or awareness to the ever-changing dynamics of the professional workplace. I've witnessed a Millennial, in the heat of a tense customer service exchange, hold up his index finger and stop someone mid-sentence to check a personal text message.

I've also seen a tech-savvy Millennial use her mobile device to rapidly address a service issue as she explained to the customer how she is solving their problem. This is where your generation has a distinct advantage if the technology can be used productively.

Each situation is different. You need to quickly decide to tolerate the situation, try to change it, or leave if you shouldn't be involved. Assessing the situation correctly before dealing with coworkers, customers, or superiors is a huge deal. People want to see positive emotion coming from you. People expect you to care about them and have facial expressions that indicate such. They want you to show empathy when the situation calls for it. Acknowledge the customer in a positive way as soon as possible in any situation.

The workplace is not high school, college, or your summer job. It is a place where you apply your education and skills in a manner that supports the overall organizational goals. Verbal and non-verbal communication is an essential element toward success, regardless of your position in the company. Experienced business professionals learn to adapt their communication styles as dictated by each situation. Too often we find entry-level workers stumped by the subtle nuances of this important dynamic. An example I often use is that of a customer service agent in his reaction to a complaint. An inexperienced agent could react as a teenage girl might when her teacher tells her to redo her homework; she lets out a sigh, pouts, rolls her eyes, and stomps her foot in frustration. The more seasoned agent will show empathy and take the customer's complaint in stride, according to the proper methods and as the situation dictates. The point is this—you need to sever the connection to the environment that accepted any form of bad situational behavior as quickly as possible, for it is not okay.

Remember these three key things depend on each situation: empathy, emotion, and energy levels. Ironically, all three of these desired behaviors are well hidden in the world of social media. About all you can do to show emotion in texting or e-mail is punch in underlines and capital letters. Although texting things like OMG in caps does show additional intensity, to me this expresses more anger than energy. Make a note: Don't do this kind of stuff when you get a real job.

Your behavior around customers or business executives will indicate to your manager that you are a team player and have a personality well suited for your position. Show excitement and enthusiasm when your manager introduces you to a new customer. Give them a positive-energy level that demonstrates you really do care.

Timing is everything. It's important to recognize the situation your employer is in before asking for personal considerations such as time off or a pay increase. A manager of a company struggling to earn profits is in no mood to hear about personal problems or the bills you have stacking up at home. Respect their time and their stress levels when engaging in that type of conversation.

There are some things that you never do in front of a customer, and things you never say. One is "It's not my fault." Another is "I didn't make the policy." A favorite is "You get what you pay for." Although the latter is a fine statement if you are in sales, it isn't if you are in customer service. The new employee may hear "you get what you pay for" and not realize when might be a good time to say it. Always choose your words carefully, and be mindful of how to deliver bad news so as not to make the situation worse.

I want you to be very aware of your verbal and non-verbal behavior. This is one of my biggest problems with some part-time jobs, the education system—where there isn't any repercussion for bad behavior—and organizations that don't offer soft-skills training. Your employer might assume you've been trained in this, and in many instances you haven't. Even some of your teachers may have failed miserably in showing appropriate emotion or giving good energy each day. If you haven't had any training in social skills or feel as if you need work in this area, ask your manager if this type of training is available. Your manager will love that you've shown the initiative.

Be mindful of how much confidence you project and when to emphasize it. For example, when selling or describing a product or service you know well, confidence is very much desired. On the other hand, show humility as the situation dictates, especially when listening to the needs of the client. When you are still learning, defer to a more experienced coworker rather than try to impress someone and get busted. The proper blend of humility and confidence is an extremely important attribute for building success. Unfortunately, it's also becoming more difficult to learn, as we do so much of our communicating via mobile devices and e-mail. Each situation varies, and knowing how to dial your level of confidence up or down is essential.

○ ○ ○

Were any of your prior jobs useful in developing your work ethic or skills?

_____

_____

_____

_____

Do you feel confident in your ability to interact with coworkers and clients?

_____

_____

_____

_____

Is your introverted or extroverted personality a good fit for the position you currently hold?

_____

_____

_____

_____

PART 3

THE SOCIAL
INFLUENCE @ HOME

Chapter 16

Attract healthy people

I f you find yourself in the middle of drama and immature conflicts on a frequent basis, it might be time to consider your social relationships both at work and outside of work. It may be who you attract, as kind people often become a magnet to lost souls. Are you one of those people that have that imaginary sign on your forehead that gives people permission to dump their problems on you? As a generous and kind person, which I assume you are, you often play the role of counselor to those who desperately seek attention. Remember how back in high school or college, certain girls always seemed to attract a certain type of boyfriend, abusive relationships, or friends who dominated or had passive-aggressive traits? These patterns extend well into your twenties and thirties. Only you can change these habits.

Without being rude, try to put some distance between yourself and the clingy coworkers who want you to either protect them or conspire with them for workplace drama. Reputation management, especially in today's world of social networking, is of vital concern. If you think about how transparent everything now is before you make your choices, you just might do things differently. You will be judged by the company you keep!

So, does misery love company? Absolutely. You will find miserable people who want to hang out with those of equal despair. If none are to be found, they come for you. Don't let depressed people bring you down to their level. Likewise, don't feel guilty being happy around them. Are you under the influence of a bad social circle or person at work? If so, get out of that situation as quickly as possible. Look to be friends with people who inspire you on some level.

Here's how to spot the troublemakers: Generally, people who cause office or social drama are people who once had a lot of attention given to them as a child or in a former job. Insecure people cause trouble because they are constantly fishing for compliments, and that often gets misunderstood by others. Former athletes, ex-models, childhood performers, and former prom queens have a hard time not being in the spotlight and struggle with this during the early stages of their careers. On the flip side, those who lacked any attention can also be a problem, because they tend to have a negative over-reaction to those who seek attention. Getting people into the middle before trouble occurs is important in the workplace, and being a part of helping management resolve the issues is an important and worthwhile stepping stone. Try to avoid being sucked into the office cliques at either end of this spectrum.

Everyone should seek advice from others no matter how old or smart you might be. It's normally wise to seek advice from trusted sources and use your filters—ethics, honesty, integrity—to vet the suggestions. A huge mistake is taking free advice from those more messed up than you. Remember that if your circle of influence isn't the place you want to be, then taking advice from people within it is just silly. Figure out quickly—through a trusted mentor, parent, or relative—who you should seek advice from before trusting those with whom you socialize. Don't get caught under the influence of a person who himself needs to seek help.

All this said, maybe you just are looking for excitement in all the wrong places. A very typical by-product of a mundane job is the need for a thrill during work hours. A better choice would be to save this for after work. The only people who you will find to play that game are others who are heading in the wrong direction. You find in every business, school, or workplace a few people who wander from room to room looking for attention, affection, or excitement, and these are the people who lack that in the evenings or weekends. Their lack of a social life is not your problem; however, it can become your problem in a hurry if you let it.

It takes years to build a reputation and only five minutes to ruin it.

Warren Buffett

○ ○ ○

Can you identify and separate yourself from unhealthy relationships?

_____

_____

_____

_____

Has the attention you've been given or earned been mostly positive or negative?

_____

_____

_____

_____

Do you have good instincts about people and filters in place?

_____

_____

_____

_____

Chapter 17

Communicate to make conflict productive

Many of the conflicts we have are simple misunderstandings based upon a lack of proper communication. Twitter is an example of a communications tool where conflicts arise from attempting to squeeze emotion and humor in 140 characters or less. Your communications strategy should be one of trying to eliminate or reducing conflict by choosing words carefully, as opposed to abbreviating them.

Conflict can take place in a positive and productive manner, and it's now considered an acceptable and healthy aspect of people working well together. The nature of being human is to have conflict and natural tensions in the workplace. I encourage you to think differently about conflict, specifically to know the difference between necessary and unnecessary conflict. In the prior chapters you read how male and female differences have an impact on conflict resolution, especially on how conflicts are resolved without lingering emotions that can create barriers to working well together. Here's the takeaway: Men see conflict as a short-term event, easily resolved and often forgotten about, whereas women see conflict as a personal attack used to belittle one another, and their feelings remain intact over longer periods of time. The key is identifying and discussing resolution and proper closure. Closure is often different for each individual. Today's managers are far better trained on conflict management that achieves true resolution and reconciliation.

Very seldom are we as smart as we think we are, and we prove that by talking instead of listening. You will find that this includes you as well. It's very easy to be driven by your own ego or the self-help motivation beliefs that we are somehow the brightest and most informed person ever. Even if that were true, it's not as important as it seems when you are just getting started. First, show much you care before you show how much you know. In the end, human compassion will outweigh the importance of proving that you are always right.

Share only useful information. If you are technical, have a sales position, or are in a role where you are explaining to customers how something works, don't overwhelm them with too much information unless they request further explanation. Knowing when to quit talking is as important as knowing what to say. The adage that you don't have to know how to butcher a pig to run a restaurant applies. By sharing unnecessary information, you may do more harm than good and talk someone out of ordering a product that was already sold. Stick to what's important to the customer, not the details you find most interesting.

Communicating effectively is somewhat of an understated talent. There is no better use of your time than to learn how to be an effective communicator. This comes in many varieties, especially speaking, listening, and writing. Having a command of the language also prevents frustration-induced outbursts brought on by a lack of good communication skills. It's why trial lawyers can bring witnesses to the breaking point and expose untold truths. They have learned the art of commanding the language and taking charge of the exchange.

Vocabulary and the command of the language is nearly a lost art. I'm thrilled when I run across a young person who can express himself in an articulate manner, make eye contact, and speak with authority on subjects he understands, then ask great questions on the topics he doesn't. Even the most tech-savvy companies can benefit from new employees who have this skill.

Don't talk just to break up the silence in the room, especially if you have no plan for what you are about to say. I describe this as nervous energy. Some people get really nervous if no one is saying anything. Unless you have been assigned by the group as the designated noisemaker, just remain silent until you have something important to contribute. As an exercise, just try waiting a few more seconds for someone else to fill that void and see how this works for you.

Have you written any type of letter recently? No, not an e-mail, but an actual letter that has the proper greeting, correct grammar, sentence structure, and salutation. Communicating in written form is time consuming but effective. As the noise floor in electronic communications elevates, the appeal of a personal letter read in a quiet setting has greater appeal.

Texting back and forth someone tricks us into believing that a conversation took place with them. I trust that you already understand that keeping your Facebook page updated and adding new pictures isn't a replacement for staying in touch with friends and family. It sure is quick and easy, but it's also an excuse for not picking up the phone and making a call. To prove this point, look at the cell phone bill of any eighteen- to thirty-year-old and check their data usage versus voice minutes. It's likely 80 percent texting versus 20 percent calling.

Communicating via sarcasm or mockery needs to be kept in check, at least until you are well-versed in the company culture. The use of sarcasm is like earning paid vacation time: You have to be there for a while before you can use it. Being sarcastic is often a carry- over bad habit from the acceptable behavior in school or a part-time job, but it seldom works to your advantage in a professional setting. Being cynical, critical of others, or especially hypocritical leaves an instant negative impression, and these are certainly not behaviors worth emulating even if they're common in your new workplace. You're not in a sitcom. Using snarky tones and eye-rolling gestures do nothing positive, and they are seldom found amusing. Separate yourself from the pack rather than joining in to get noticed.

The single biggest problem in communication is the illusion that it has taken place.

George Bernard Shaw

○ ○ ○

How does your vocabulary, choice of words, writing styles, and methods of communication rate within your organization?

_____

_____

_____

_____

Has texting, tweeting, or other social methods caused you to avoid just picking up the phone and talking to people?

_____

_____

_____

_____

Does e-mail get you in trouble on occasion?

_____

_____

_____

_____

Chapter 18

Understand that the best things in life aren't things

Most twentysomethings can't imagine how a rich or famous person could ever be unhappy. So why do you suppose high-profile people end up in rehab or going through multiple divorces? My suspicion is that very wealthy people with outrageous possessions become addicted to acquiring more and more things in order to get a new rush with each purchase. The quicker they add a new thing, the faster they become bored with an old one. Pretty soon nothing excites them. They are caught up in an endless cycle of devaluing the old and coveting the new—not a life worth living or to envy.

So what then are the best things? Some people argue that it's the freedom we enjoy, some say it's the love we share for our family and friends, others believe it's the faith they have in life everlasting, and others suggest it's having limitless choices. The choices are what confuse us. Money allows for more choices in how we live and how we spend our time. Depending on the person, it is just as hard to have money as not to have it. Chasing financial success at the expense of other things is a dangerous proposition, but it's becoming so difficult to raise a family with even the basic necessities without a median level of income. Being rich is a very subjective matter.

Do more things just bring more headaches? I've heard it said before that the **real measure of our wealth is how much we'd be worth if we lost all our money.** That makes you wonder if people in poverty-stricken areas who lost all their belongings in natural disasters actually suffer as much as people who have huge houses and lots of valuables. I tend to believe that having material things will only bring happiness if they serve a purpose. I subscribe to the notion that if we are thankful for what we have, we will end up having more, whereas if we dwell on what we don't have, we will never end up with enough.

I'm starting to see a trend toward minimalist behavior in many young people. This may be a temporary condition stemming from our weak economy, or maybe it's a new measure of self-control that young couples are adopting—I'm not sure. Either way, the idea of living within your means is a very positive sign. It may also be an indication that young people are realistic about reduced-job opportunities and higher unemployment, which gives them the freedom to pack and up move if they lose their jobs. Mobility then becomes a component of achieving financial stability. This is a very important discussion worth having with your spouse.

In Psychology 101, Abraham Maslow's hierarchy of needs is taught. That principle, first introduced in 1943, still rings true even in the age of technology and social networking. It describes a path that begins at the very basic physiological needs like food and shelter, safety and security, and a sense of belonging, and eventually progresses throughout life to a level of self-actualization. When following this progression, we can achieve milestones where self-esteem, a strong sense of belonging, and unwavering commitment to our core values take place in a natural and sequential order. This all occurs prior to really knowing and realizing any true measure of success. If success somehow happens too soon or too easy, self-destruction is quite likely.

Medical experts are now beginning to realize that people under the social influence are being lured into groups in order to achieve a sense of belonging and self-worth. This leads to a loss of sleep, an addiction to check sites throughout the day, monitor Twitter constantly, and the like. Eighty-four percent of smartphone users report using their phone as an alarm clock, and 65 percent of smartphone users report checking text messages as the last thing they do before bedtime. These behaviors are a sure sign that you are under the influence and need to make changes.

In addition to being impatient, there are so many new obstacles that can trip us up and derail our lives' natural progression. Social addictions can create misplaced priorities, and the need for instant gratification and a false sense of belonging can cause us to stumble. As an impatient society, it is very typical for the aggressive and competitive Millennial to try to skip these steps and race to the top before he or she is ready. That could mean starting a business before being really prepared. It could be overextending a credit line. It could be an ego- or pride-driven get-rich scheme. The important lesson is that sometimes we just don't know what we don't know, and only time and experience will prove this. Circumvention of the steps needs to be carefully considered from every angle.

I suggest that you do an audit of the things you have and the things you want on occasion, and, as you age, evaluate how much your priorities have changed. The older we get, the more *time* becomes the new currency. Young people place a high value on money, because it allows them to buy more stuff, whereas old people look to have more time in order to enjoy the stuff they bought. Living within your means at each stage of life and having enough time with friends and family may be the thing you really need. If using social media allows you more time for enjoyment of these steps, then I'm all for it.

What is necessary to change a person is to change his awareness of himself.

Abraham Maslow

☐ ☐ ☐

Are you able to live comfortably on the income you currently earn?

_____

_____

_____

_____

If not, is your first instinct to look for a new job, or cut back on expenses?

_____

_____

_____

_____

Are you realistic, patient, and thoughtful regarding the steps to financial stability?

_____

_____

_____

_____

Chapter 19

Give and save before you spend

When we think of money, we think of how we will spend it—on ourselves. Somehow, we are good at that, or maybe it comes naturally. What isn't as natural for most people is the idea of giving a percentage of that money to the things we believe in most, such as church and charities. It all begins with establishing a budget for spending, saving, and giving. With every paycheck, every month, every year, giving that money becomes a way of life can to happiness and fulfillment.

Start giving and saving early! I find it fascinating that we see financial security continuously ranked very high in the list of priorities for Millennial workers, yet when asked about investing, they seem disinterested. Most say they want to make a lot of money and focus on just that as the best way to achieve their financial goals. Too few young professionals understand that saving a percentage of their income early in life will lead to financial security when they're older. They want to acquire cars, houses, clothes, and more stuff now, figure out how to pay them off, and then worry about retirement savings later.

If your employer offers a deferred savings or retirement plan, contribute at least 5 percent of your pre-tax income to it. More important than the actual dollar amount of your savings is the culture of savings that you are developing for yourself. Eventually, it will become a larger nest egg and, hopefully, a way to build financial independence and not have to be dependent or burdensome on others.

Financial independence is a process measured over time. It takes discipline, and if you are married, a shared belief of the importance in starting early. Many married couples have a different outlook on savings. One is generally the more fiscally responsible and conservative partner, the other more geared toward living paycheck to paycheck. Seldom do couples have the exact same mindset on savings, giving, and spending. Most couples say the single biggest source of arguments in young married couples is money related. Knowing this makes it crucial to have a mutually agreed upon plan in place early on so you don't battle one another for years to come. Even if you are single, keep a clean credit history—your future spouse may see excessive debt as a deal breaker.

If you are not in a financial position to give money to your favorite cause, volunteering your time and talents can be just as effective and rewarding. Once you find yourself in the right place financially, then embrace the concept of "radical generosity." This giving-back concept comes after the basic necessities of life, family needs, savings, and other expenses and savings are accounted for. It's the belief that we have an obligation to provide for others and create an environment that is better than how we found it. This could be a future goal. I caution you not to start too early or too late in life.

○ ○ ○

Have you started investing for the future, college funds, etc.?

_____

_____

_____

_____

Does volunteering, making contributions, or becoming involved in the community interest you?

_____

_____

_____

_____

Chapter 20

Earn more than you spend; save more than you borrow

So easy to say and so hard to do! It's a basic and fundamental principle of being on your own. Young people today want desperately to sever their financial ties to their parents or grandparents, yet struggle to maintain a lifestyle they now simply cannot afford. Codependent children are entering the workforce in record numbers and maintaining that status well beyond marriage and well into their thirties. Here's why: smartphones, iTunes, satellite TV, satellite radio, cable TV, car payments, insurance, housing costs, utilities, student loans, etc., etc. are simply out of control. So we do the worst thing possible—charge all of this to a credit card. What do we do when that gets maxed out? We get another credit card.

Things have dramatically changed in just one generation. From the list mentioned above, only housing costs, utilities, and maybe a car payment were part of the norm a generation ago. We have somehow allowed the line between luxury and necessity to become blurred. It would be an interesting conversation to have with your parents or grandparents to compare how they spent their money at your age versus the items you spend your earnings on, and most importantly, how these items support your quality of life goals.

Debt versus savings ratios are also spiraling out of control. According to the Bureau of Labor Statistics a 2010 survey of recent college graduates found that 27 percent of these twenty-two-year-olds would be considered financially literate. Likewise, the Council for Education Economics revealed that in 2011, only 13 percent of high school students were required to take a personal economics class in high school. It's very clear that there's a fundamental weakness in educating the new generation of workers about money management and even knowing what metrics and financial ratios they should be watching. That lack of education has caused many reckless spending habits to form, created dismal credit scores, and placed millions of people in their early twenties into the ChexSystems database. Being placed on this national credit watch list can haunt you for years. Even opening a new checking account in a different city can be a major problem.

It is well documented that the majority of young people have more credit card, student loan, and personal debt than they do savings. Today's twenty-something's hold an average debt of $45,000, of which the majority is in credit cards. If you are unable to manage your credit card debt, you must seek financial advice from a friend or parent outside the banking world. Remember what banks sell and how they make their money. Excessive debt needs to be managed quickly if that is a problem for you. Overspending for non-essential items that require excessive debt-to-income ratios always leads to unhappiness.

Never go to your employer with the sad story of living paycheck to paycheck and not able to make ends meet. If he or she knows you have three cars, a motorcycle, student loans, kids in private school, DirecTV plus cable, and just came back from Hawaii, you will get no sympathy. This is not their problem.

If you have access to a 401k or other savings program that allows pretax money to be placed in a long-term savings program, get started as soon as you can. That is for your future, not to be borrowed against. It can become the start of what you will eventually have to offset debt. The key is to build up your savings plan and pay down your debt, every month, every year. Every time you see your bank statement, ask yourself if you have too much house, too much car, and too much debt. Those three combined items are at the root of most Millennials' financial woes.

Be a smart borrower. Do yourself a huge favor, and understand how interest rates impact your monthly payments. Borrowing money to purchase something that depreciates rapidly, like a new car, isn't smart. In two years, most new cars will be worth about half of what you paid. Your loan value will be more than the car is worth as soon as you drive off in it. Instead, look for a certified preowned car with a transferable warranty. Let someone in a better financial position take the hit on the depreciation.

When you buy your first home, save at least 20 percent for the down payment. Regardless of what the bank tells you, wait until you have this in order to compensate for unforeseen market fluctuations. In addition to the down payment, be prepared to invest money into the house because things will need to be repaired and updated. A standard rule of thumb: Stash away six months of living expenses as a rainy day fund. It is far more important to have this than it is to have another car payment, extravagant vacations, or other luxuries. As a contingency, this may be a huge benefit if a job situation changes unexpectedly.

Never borrow money for nonessential items. Use debit, not credit. Vacations and toys should be paid for in cash. Credit cards are a nightmare. They are like crack for undisciplined consumers. Carry two cards maximum. Avoid store cards no matter how good the introductory offer. Build up a great credit score and try as hard as you can to pay your cards off on a regular basis. Save and use a debit card, not credit cards.

○ ○ ○

Have you done any type of financial plan?

_____

_____

_____

_____

Do you budget or track your monthly expenses compared to income?

_____

_____

_____

_____

What do you generally use: debit or credit?

_____

_____

_____

_____

Chapter 21

Don't just raise children; raise future adults

One of the most challenging stages in your career comes when you are a working parent. It will cause numerous conflicts, guilt, and tension, at home and at work. At times it will seem impossible, but you will figure it out. Actually you will figure it out when you realize that it is virtually impossible to be a perfect parent and a perfect employee simultaneously. Manageable compromises must be made and communicated effectively.

When the additional income of two working parents collides with the guilt of imperfection, overcompensation occurs. We tend to buy our kids affection at that point. There really is no need for doing that. By the way, kids are very smart about laying the guilt trip on you so you will buy them more stuff. A better approach is to use the additional income earned for savings, retirement planning, and college funding.

We all want our kids to have a better life than we did; but when you raise kids, you just get larger kids. Along the way, hundreds of teachable moments present themselves that can shape their adult life. For example, teaching by example when you demonstrate the difference between paying with credit as opposed to saving up for a nonessential item can be quite influential on a child. Years later, they think debit card before credit card.

Busy adults confuse children with poor or unfinished explanations. For instance, look at the way we teach them about technology. We are so thrilled when they learn to guide their way through an early learning program, yet we scold them for going to the Internet. We want them to attend the finest schools with the latest technology, but we forbid them from using social media sites. Kids don't understand the risk/reward proposition of the digital world unless we explain to them why boundaries are necessary. Time is one important boundary. I've said many times to parent groups that if you simply require your student to put in the same time on academics as they do TV, games, and social media, they will turn out just fine.

Excessive coddling will lead to codependent children. They become codependent adults, which is basically the same thing as a very large child. The "gimmes" become more expensive. Their age is the only indicator of adulthood. At some point, you are doing your children a huge disservice by trying to help financially. Granted, there are times and situations that make perfect sense to invest in their future, such as in a quality education. Appreciation for your support versus expecting a handout is the mindset that needs to be established. Expectation, or a sense of birthright, leads to a lack of a work ethic that can span an entire lifetime. If you come from a wealthy family, it is best to keep that information under wraps until you earn the respect of others for your performance and work ethic. Flaunting it backfires every time.

Having childlike, codependent young adults in the workforce makes no one happy. No one is proud of what takes place: Relationships with siblings suffer, and quite often the bad habits they learn carry over to the workplace. This carryover leads to marginal behavior, job-hopping, lack of self-esteem, and a tendency to run away from conflict rather than solving problems. They come to work expecting the company to "take care" of them.

Placing a financial safety net underneath your child can seem like a great thing, but without proper direction and clear expectations, it can become a real problem as they begin a new career. We have to teach them at an early age that the government, their employer, and even their parents are not there to take care of them once they become adults.

Employers can spot the kid "born on third base" a mile away—that is, unless parents teach them to start their first job as if they were still in the batter's box, not even to first base yet. Those third base kids have had a life of privilege and can be awesome employees with the proper guidance. That is as long as the parents don't screw them up by teaching them their wealth or status somehow entitles them to bypass the hard work required in their new job. As a parent, I totally believe that children of privilege should be guided to do as much community service work as possible to gain as deep a sense of humility and respect for others as possible.

Regarding respect: Kids do as they see you doing. In your workplace you can demonstrate professional respect for your company or choose not to. When you come home with words of disrespect for your supervisor or speak badly about the company in front of the kids, the message translates to children that it must be okay to demonstrate disrespect for an authority figure.

Teachers and coaches have come to bear the brunt of disrespect when parents demonstrate disrespect for their authority figures. Being respectful of people you come in contact with while your child is observing will translate into raising a young adult who will show great respect for others. What better gift than this can we pass onto our children?

New parents, if your son or daughter is in a sport, please be mindful of your sideline behavior. I've seen some horrible displays of overzealous parents attempting to straighten out the officials and coaches, only to drive their children to the point of quitting. This is a lasting impression, and if you think for a minute that your children don't remember and learn from your bad behavior, you are dead wrong. If you can't control this, then it's best to stay home.

Your children will blow through the money you leave them. Respect and work ethic will last them a lifetime.

Just like managers at work, parents struggle to find positive ways to administer consequences. Great parents discipline their children because they love them and want them to not repeat the mistake. Getting control of the families' technology habit is a good example of discipline and consequences. Children truly do not understand why their parents can be glued to Facebook and they can't. If it's so dangerous, then why is Mom doing it? Sadly, many parents end up dishing out the punishment in the heat of an emotional and complicated situation such as this by engaging in a shouting match, followed by a stern "because I said so." Obviously, there are dozens of more constructive explanations and discipline methods that will be more effective.

Be aware of this pattern: An out of control ten-year-old will soon become an out of control eighteen-year-old and then an out of control employee. They won't just naturally grow out of a defiance phase. Parents who deny poor behavior spotted early will only make matters far worse after years of acting up has been allowed to continue. For example, truancy in school will equate to poor punctuality and missing work. Aggression at school will equate to creating unnecessary conflict at work. Acceptance of poor grades will equate to accepting mediocre reviews. Dropping classes will equate to job-hopping. Bad behavior spotted early needs to be corrected. Your influence on the type of adult that your child will soon become is huge!

◻ ◻ ◻

Do you and your spouse have similar parenting approaches and discipline philosophies?

_____

_____

_____

_____

Are you mindful of showing respect to authority figures around your children?

_____

_____

_____

_____

What patterns and habits do you need to correct before the children imitate that behavior?

_____

_____

_____

PART 4

MOVING FORWARD

Chapter 22

Get ahead by working hard

There is no substitute for hard work. I'm an Iowa Hawkeyes football fanatic. The Hawkeyes have a reputation of getting more out of student athletes than most other programs, which is vital because the recruiting challenges here are greater. To reinforce the need for outworking the competition, they have this message on a sign as you enter the locker room: Hard work and a positive attitude will beat talent every time, if talent doesn't work hard. That is true on the courts and playing fields, as well as in the workplace. Opportunity presents itself every day to the seemingly Average Joe when the superstar ahead of them becomes bored with doing what he determines to be ordinary and boring work.

Job-hopping may seem like a method to get ahead, but it will lead to a messy résumé and employers questioning your loyalty. Too often, young college graduates entering the workforce are given advice to "start out" at a company and keep moving around. This is bad advice most of the time.

Somewhere, sometime you will have an opportunity to show that your hard work and passion for what you do will prove more valuable than raw talent. You have to focus on overachieving and not giving up on yourself when it would be easy to do so. There will also be times that you get frustrated and think, "I am just going to do enough to get by." Those are the pivotal moments or decision points when only you can determine what will happen next. Remember this simple formula: If you choose as your maximum effort to do only the required minimum, the sum total of your life will be mediocrity. Somewhere along the line, the people you most admire, respect, and want to pattern your life after have pushed through decision points like these just as you can.

Have you ever thought that maybe it would be easier to work as little as possible and just get by? Forget the stress, headaches, sleepless nights, and emotional rollercoaster of performance highs and lows. If you have, stop to think about your pride and dignity. Think back to those people who inspired you at an early age. How would they respond to that struggle? They absolutely had those difficult moments, yet somehow they fought through them. You wouldn't even remember that teacher or coach's name today if they didn't get past their bad moments. They were there for you then. They can't be here today, but they did leave you with something special, and you must decide for yourself how to take what they taught and apply it to this current situation. Life is filled with these challenging times.

Getting ahead regardless of natural talent requires a desire to win. Showing a boss or coach the desire to win is far more important than telling them how much education, talent, or skills you might have. Even in an initial first meeting, the most important impression you can leave is how much desire you have to succeed. If you feel your presence in conversations or discussions seem insignificant, study the subject matter, and be ready to contribute. Too often we beg for the right to speak, only to discover we haven't much to say. Be better prepared than the next person.

One day you will learn that the greatest obstacle to your success will be your own fear—primarily the fear of taking a chance and failing. At some point, you need to overcome that and bet on yourself to succeed, rather than assume you will fail if you try for a promotion or stretch yourself to learn a new skill. It's not a lack of education or a time commitment issue that holds you back; it's your own fear of trying and failing. People who learn to overcome that fear early in their career, rather than looking back and reflecting on the lost opportunities, will find success even if they try and fail on occasion.

In my experience I have found two primary behaviors that can hold people back. The first is projecting a sense of fear brought on by a lack of confidence, insecurity, and excuses. We learn from failure, and the best part of trying and failing is that the next time will be easier. It sounds corny, but you really do need to be willing to fail in order to find success. The second is an unwillingness to do the occasional task or fill in for others when the work appears to be beneath you. It seems counterintuitive, but you can really get ahead and impress others if you are willing to pitch in and help in projects and tasks that need to be completed for the overall good of the business. It may be the best way to get ahead.

I've witnessed firsthand an interesting dynamic that confuses the new generation of workers. It has to do with the ingrained notion of being a confident person. Your parents may have raised you to be independent, self-sufficient, and exude confidence, in which case accepting criticism and accepting the guidance of others is very difficult. On the other hand, you may lean in the other direction where a fear of failure is driven by the lack of confidence. I've found that people in the middle seem to be best at asking to be mentored and even asking for help and guidance. As they say, behind every successful person is someone who has offered their support. Try hard to accept this if offered to you by a trusted source.

To get yourself in the right frame of mind as you get to work, think this way about the day: The start of the day is all about possibilities, and the end of the day is all about results. This covers about every workplace situation and occupation. It is important to know that you have each day to show results, and that each day offers new possibilities that give you a better chance at producing positive results.

Good bosses do notice people making an effort to get ahead. Nine times out of ten, the employee with a superior work ethic will get noticed and considered for advancement above all others. Following the rules is very important, and it will keep you employed. Understanding how to act as the owner would in the absence of clearly defined rules will make you a superstar. The very best way to get ahead is to continually improve upon these three essentials attributes:

1. Ethics
2. Education
3. Exceptional communications and customer service skills

〇 〇 〇

Can you pinpoint any one thing that is holding you back?

_____

_____

_____

_____

Does the fear of making mistakes keep you from trying?

_____

_____

_____

_____

Are you willing to put in the extra effort and do the heavy lifting?

_____

_____

_____

_____

Chapter 23

Use your secret weapon

Traditional, conservative middle-age people like me often carry on about the shortcomings of the next generation as we see how easily distracted you are, blaming technology for this. I see a strength, however, that is often overlooked by everyone, and that strength is the uncanny ability of a Millennial to multitask—to tend to many applications and processes simultaneously. So as you were playing video games, updating your Facebook page, tweeting, and talking on your cell phone during dinner, you were learning to partition your thoughts into compartments. Now that you've matured, try to hone the underlying talent it took to be proficient at performing multiple tasks into useable workplace skills. This can set you apart in a fast-paced work environment.

Multitasking is a huge asset to have in many occupations. To many in my generation, multitasking is like New York City traffic is to a farm kid. It's overwhelming and unimaginable how to navigate the city with all the commotion, noise, and the rapid pace. To the Millennial, however, multitasking is the norm. I use the comparison to traffic because if you've lived in

New York your entire life you would know of nothing else. You expect traffic, noise, and the pace to be that way everywhere. The distinct advantage you have is using these skills for the benefit of your employer once you get a job that can leverage this talent.

If multitasking is your secret weapon, here's your Kryptonite: idle time. The workplace isn't always going to be a high energy, fast paced flurry of activity. There usually is calm before the storm, moments of idle time at the start or end of the day, the times when others screw off. What you do in your idle time to provide value to an employer is equally as important as what you do during the busiest moments. Going to your supervisor with thoughtful and strategic methods for using your multitasking skills for the benefit of the company during this time is huge. It can be something that really sets you apart from the others.

Use this superhero skill as a weapon for good, not for evil. Use this to establish yourself as an employee of high value because you are from this generation, not to fritter away idle time at the workplace. Prove to your manager or owner that you are a great employee because you can do so many things well, and you can keep everything straight as you do them. Show your manager how to leverage the skills you have with social media to help him grow the business. You have mastered the art of driving engagement and just may not realize how it could apply to the customer base of your organization. This is a true strength of your generation.

A highly valuable and often overlooked asset of today's new multitasking workforce is the ability to keep the many layers of information and methods of communication aligned. Multitasking is natural to you because you mastered it as a teen, and now you think nothing of these chaotic situations. One thing to remember though is that the steady stream of information coming at you has a tendency to skew your sense of timing. By that I mean knowing when to push information out and when to react to situations. Think a couple of steps ahead before hitting the send button. Immediately retweeting in order to be the first one to share news can be dangerous. What's more important over the long haul: acting or thinking?

Stay focused. Unlike college, where you could blow off studying to play video games all day, work has to come before playtime. Toggling back and forth between work and play during the workday isn't an option. Save it for later, and fight off the distractions that take away from your productivity at work.

Be patient. You are very quick and efficient at writing an e-mail, tweeting, and getting a message out there. That does not mean you should expect the other person to respond quickly. It is frustrating to a Millennial worker when you write this beautiful e-mail, hit send, and then have to wait for a response. This is hard to imagine, but business people don't always stay logged in to every app like you do. They may do business e-mails once a day and close their browser the rest of the time. Use good judgment before resending. There is no requirement for the person receiving a text or e-mail to respond.

Can you multitask effectively and in a positive fashion?

_____

_____

_____

_____

Are you able to use social platforms without compromising real conversations and interpersonal interaction?

_____

_____

_____

_____

Chapter 24

Restore and replenish

How well do you bounce back from being stressed out and overbooked? Think about this question when having your quiet "mountaintop" moment on your next day off from work. Resilient and positive-minded people can see the good in every situation. They choose to focus on a positive outcome and what life will be like when the bad situation is over. They don't complain about what is happening, but rather they choose to describe how much better it will be down the road once the problem goes away.

Negative thinking eats away at the core of people. It tends to drain the spirit of hope and a brighter future from those who dwell on the negative or who surround themselves with negative-thinking people. Try restoring yourself by being positive about every disappointing situation. Try seeing the light at the end and focusing on what you can do to make things better, not on why they are currently so bad. Instead of complaining about today, try being excited about tomorrow.

Not everyone is successful at their first career choice or for that matter, makes a good choice when they've accepted their first job. Thousands of people get through college to find out they can't find a job in their desired field of work. They take whatever they can find, struggle to tolerate the daily grind, and show no passion for the work. This is a problem. You won't be successful, and the reference from this employer will be bad. Please know this—you can't be very good at something you hate. Also know that everyone eventually finds something they enjoy and will be good at—and you will as well. Even if you don't succeed at the first thing, eventually you will find something you are very good at and will succeed.

If you find yourself in this situation, go straight to your boss and explain how you feel. Be totally honest and upfront about this situation with him or her and see what other possibilities might exist. The best thing may be for you to agree on a timeframe for leaving the organization, and if it happens with this level of honesty, this could actually produce a good letter of recommendation and a positive reference for your ethical behavior. You can rebound nicely from this if handled properly.

Use your vacation time wisely. If you get paid time off, use it to restore and replenish. Don't use your vacation time to engage in even more stressful activities than your work and then need to relax and unwind when you get back to work. Give yourself a buffer day back at home before returning to your job. A good vacation choice might be something like going to Vegas and winning or losing a couple of hundred bucks. A great vacation is going to Vegas and observing the magnitude of the Grand Canyon and Hoover Dam.

People who are living under the social influence have a very hard time powering down their technology and what they perceive to be their lifeline to the outside world. Try hard to disconnect from technology if that is a big part of your job. Staying connected to a stressful environment isn't doing anything to help you recharge. Likewise, if you have an addiction to Twitter or Facebook, set them aside for the week. Don't update, post, or tweet that you will be gone, just limit the use to a few minutes each day. You can tell people all about the vacation when you get home.

Don't ever use your paid time off for the purpose of exploring a new job. This will ultimately lead to a pattern of job-hopping. Paid time off, or vacation time, is a benefit provided by your current employer. They are paying you to be gone, relax, and come back better than when you left. Use it for your benefit and the benefit of your employer, but never use it against them.

Perhaps overscheduling is the big issue. If so, start saying no upfront rather than always apologizing for under-delivering. What thing can you give up or delegate to others that would make the day or week more manageable? Take that first one off the schedule and look for the next. Simplifying your schedule will give you the one thing we can make more of, and that is time. Time available to focus on more important activities should be worth more to you than anything else.

Maybe the ordinary clutter is what drives you crazy. Do you simply have too much stuff you don't ever use or need? Does having this stuff really make sense? Does cleaning, dusting, moving, and storing ordinary stuff you probably don't use take up valuable time and space? Unless it's really meaningful, rid yourself of useless material items and any unnecessary time-consuming activities.

I am not judged by the number of times I fail, but by the number of times I succeed; and the number of times I succeed is in direct proportion to the number of times I can fail and keep on trying.

Tom Hopkins, author and speaker

○ ○ ○

Does negative thinking and assuming the worst affect your everyday life?

_____

_____

_____

_____

Can you eliminate any low-priority time wasters that impede accomplishing the important things in your day?

_____

_____

_____

_____

Are you experiencing a lack of sleep, too much stress, or too many hours at work to be effective?

_____

_____

_____

_____

Chapter 25

Develop emotional IQ in the post-dodgeball era

Without the cruel lessons we once learned by playing dodgeball, it's pretty easy to forget we have shortcomings. Today in competitive activities, we minimize winning and losing in order to reward effort, attendance, and punctuality. It wasn't always that way, as my generation experienced harsher lessons early in life. Yet for some reason, school seems harder, and the mean kids have found new methods of dishing out punishment.

There is no participation trophy given in the business world for just showing up on time. We are seeing a wave of young people entering the workforce who have never experienced the agony of defeat in their youth. From this arise situations where a supervisor may be the first to ever ask for a change in behavior or deliver a bad evaluation for performance.

A few months ago, a friend and industry leader told me a story about a new employee coming in for his first job review. Noticeably uncomfortable, the young man asked about his performance and how he was doing. The manager gave him some great feedback, some good feedback, and then some areas for improvement. He used a grading scale where "1" indicated the need for improvement and "5" denoted excellence.

The manager gave the young man a "2" in one category, and when he realized that compared to a D in school he began to cry right on the spot. You see, this young man had been a straight-A student in high school and college, and he had never received a bad grade in anything before. Actually, he had never received bad news of any type before. He was unprepared to hear anything negative about himself. This young man was told from early on that he was an exceptional athlete, student, musician, part-time employee, and so forth. It gets worse.

The very next day, the manager received a phone call from this highly celebrated young man's mother. His mother was furious that he had given her boy a bad review, and she demanded an explanation. As you can imagine, this didn't go over well with the manager, and the young man's career began to unravel from there.

Under no circumstances is this acceptable behavior in any professional workplace. You have to fight your own battles with your emotions in check. It is perfectly acceptable to seek the advice of a mentor, trusted coworker, or parent, but you are the party responsible for the advancement of your career. Don't ask friends or family to fight your battles once you become an adult.

A bad review isn't always a crisis situation, and in most cases when it becomes a crisis, it's due to the overreaction of an employee who is unaccustomed to hearing anything bad about themselves. At times like these—gut-checking, character-building moments—it is crucial to keep your emotions in check. Stay in control, remain calm, and think rationally. Even more important is to listen to the advice given by the person doing the review. Now is not the time to be defiant or refuse to believe that you may have areas to improve upon. Fix the problem and move on.

Keeping anger under control is absolutely essential in the workplace. Projecting anger toward others will quickly raise the red flag. Emotional situations can trigger even the calmest of people to throw a temper tantrum or become visibly angry. Aggressive gestures, inappropriate written communication, and volume and tone of voice are all grounds for termination. If you find yourself even remotely falling into this category or have experienced this behavior, please seek the underlying cause with a professional. Regardless of the situation, this has to be kept in check.

◯ ◯ ◯

How well do you handle your emotions when you receive bad news?

_____

_____

_____

_____

In relationship to others your age, how do you place in maturity level?

_____

_____

_____

_____

Chapter 26

Learn from adversity

L ife isn't fair, and it is going to throw you many curve balls. Adversity can bring forth the most remarkable stories and life lessons. These lessons shape how we make decisions, and they allow us to become better at our jobs and even as parents. Adversity is an unfamiliar concept to many Millennials. It's also difficult to accept criticism and allow yourself to be instructed by people from a generation who you don't feel are in touch with the new economy and technologies of today. Those who accept the wisdom of the older generation and learn to appreciate their perspective can often get ahead faster than those who come in convinced they need to change the status quo.

Mistakes are acceptable if done while showing initiative, and if they are not repeated. One of the more frustrating things about business is that mistakes are often repeated by distracted younger workers. The adversity and conflict that arise from these mistakes have to be owned by those involved. As we are now being encouraged by educators to break the rules and make radical change happen, we sometimes find ourselves sideways with the boss who established these rules. Challenging the status quo is one thing, breaking the rules in order to get ahead is very different. Knowing which is which is crucial. Perseverance is the key to overcoming the setbacks suffered by making costly mistakes. Learn to be patient and not expect too much too soon.

Every boss knows the difference between employees who try hard to improve a process and fail versus someone who repeats mistakes. Success most often follows a number of failures from someone seeking to improve their business. Very few companies will punish someone who gives their all to make an improvement and fails. Over time, you won't be judged by the number of times you fail. You will be measured by the extra effort you put in, the results it produces, and the number of times you find success after you fail.

I've witnessed many mistakes being made, with situational awareness at its very best and at its very worst on many occasions. Crisis management is part of life and something we all learn to deal with. I've had some crazy travel experiences that enabled me to make observations of how people behave in crisis situations. The positive and negative side of people come out, which gives valuable insight into behaviors like decision making, showing kindness to others, and making first impressions.

I recall one such experience being stuck in a minivan cab for seven hours during a hurricane in New Orleans. On this day, I met some fascinating people from all over the world, stuck in a city that had basically shut down. I was lucky to get a cab driven by a very bright young man, a recent graduate from Tulane University. He worked so hard to get me back to the airport, yet every roadway was flooded. He had obviously never been in that situation before, and he had no idea what to do. This young man demonstrated excellent customer service skills throughout the adverse situation. He tried everything he could to get me on my way out of town.

Together we found out that once the meter hits $200, it stops. His concern wasn't about the fee: It was how to get me somewhere safely. We came across several flooded cabs with stranded passengers, and each time we asked if we could stop and help them. Before long, we had a cab full of stranded visitors, including a honeymooning couple, male and female world-class body builders, and a gourmet chef. As the dispatchers all left for home, they told the young cab driver he was on his own. This young man, who grew up in New Orleans, offered to show us other parts of the city.

We had an incredible backstreet tour of New Orleans, stopped several times for beverages, stopped at some music clubs, saw people's belongings floating down the streets, heard some crazy stories, and shared a great day together. This young man showed perseverance in the face of adversity. He missed a final exam that day, we all missed our flights, and by the time we got situated in a non-flooded hotel, we all learned a lesson in overcoming adversity. The young man refused to be paid anything after this seven-hour ordeal, as he claimed to have had his best day ever from the life lessons this provided him. This kid slept in his cab, and the next morning he showed up early and gave us all a ride back to the airport. How many twenty-two-year-olds would do that? We tipped him $300. He was exactly the type of person every employer would hire in an instant. Adversity was what brought this out in him.

I've also developed a real soft spot for flight attendants and gate agents. I've seen far more bad behavior from adults than I have from children when traveling. It takes time and maturity to realize that you have no control over travel delays and cancellations. The airline industry employee's deal with adversity caused by situations they too don't control, and yet they bear the brunt of uninformed travelers who somehow must believe the gate agents can go out and fix the plane. Unrealistic expectations can cause a firestorm of rage and emotion that needs to be kept under control regardless of how badly you need to be somewhere. If you travel in your new job, by all means learn to travel well.

Be prepared for unexpected delays and cancellations. Especially if traveling with your boss or a coworker, act properly and be respectful of others. Show that you can cope with adversity in every situation and be under control emotionally when adversity presents itself. When the crisis is over, assess your performance under duress and even ask others how well you handled the situation or what actions would have been better.

The greatest glory in living lies not in never falling, but in rising every time we fall.

Nelson Mandela

○ ○ ○

Do you tend to fall apart, or rise above when faced with adversity?

_____

_____

_____

_____

Do you control your emotions in the event of schedule disruptions?

_____

_____

_____

_____

Do you prefer to be in control of a situation or to let others take charge?

_____

_____

_____

_____

Chapter 27

Establish priorities worth keeping

C learly there are differences in the priorities we have depending on age. There may be some common ground, though that remains true regardless of the age differences between your friends, family, and coworkers. Most everyone places a high priority on being a great parent someday. Talking about being a great parent is a worthwhile conversation to have with every person you meet. However, questioning coworkers' parenting skills is never an appropriate work conversation. Observe others to find out what type of parent you want to be.

Human kindness and just being a genuine and good person should always be a priority and spans all generations. Allow yourself to be mentored. I really encourage young people to find a "work parent," especially if your family life was a bit dysfunctional. It can be a true friendship and a mentoring relationship that will last forever and help you navigate the obstacles with your new career. If you find that great mentor, listen carefully and use their advice to shape your career.

Another priority that is intergenerational is maintaining a healthy marriage and family life. Even single people rank that as a top priority for themselves one day. Doing the right things, even before finding a future spouse, is important, as is where you might be looking for that future spouse. Recently, I spoke to a young man who was in his late twenties and expressed frustration in not finding the right type of woman with whom he could settle down. Upon my inquiries, I found out that about the only place he ever socialized with his friends was at a local strip joint. How strange that he couldn't find a nice, wholesome girl there. Make family a priority, even before you start one of your own.

We are absolutely in a transformation of technology, and we will experience many new ways where technology will shape our lives. Mobile, virtual, visual, and social technologies will have great impact on us personally and professionally. During this transformation it is important to stay grounded in the priorities we have set for ourselves. For example, if we have new technology that enables us to do a video conference instead of visiting our relatives, is that really the same? Can we create the same experience as we intended, or are we altering our behavior and making sacrifices in our priorities? New technology has a way of sneaking up on you, getting you addicted to the convenience, and then testing your commitment to personal interaction. Keep personal interaction between friends and family a top priority.

Everything seems like a priority to the person who has an overcomplicated life. Trust me, it's not. I've said hundreds of times to people I've mentored that family always comes before business. It's a priority worth keeping. Now, if you find that you say that yourself, yet your actions don't support it, you need to begin the disentanglement process. Do what you can to sustain those priorities that truly define who you are, and disentangle yourself from commitments that may be somewhat important, but not most important.

○ ○ ○

Are your priorities ranked and do you live by that ranking?

_____

_____

_____

_____

Have you shared your priorities and core values with others?

_____

_____

_____

_____

Are you willing to put these priorities to the test if need be?

_____

_____

_____

_____

Chapter 28

Be more human

Treating people with mutual respect, showing care and concern, and providing empathy every day, every week, and every year will guide your life in many positive ways. It's important to remember that most people have struggles we don't know about and can't see. Be kinder than you have to, as you just never know what problems your friends and coworkers may be hiding. Treating everyone you meet as if they were the most important person you know will ultimately bring you happiness while providing a lasting impression. Treatment of others begins to define who you are. Defining who you are will eventually lead you to the best lifestyle for you. Knowing what that lifestyle is and committing to it will allow you to slow down in areas you need to and speed up in others. Simplifying isn't just slowing down, it's self-regulating the speed in which you make the journey.

I've tried my best to practice random acts of kindness for fifteen-plus years. In all that time, I can remember being taken advantage of only once. At my home airport I saw a sobbing mother with three young children at baggage claim. She was trying to rent a car around midnight, and her credit card wouldn't go through for the additional car seats she forgot to reserve. Company policy required the agent not to let her leave without car seats. With a long drive ahead of her, the holidays quickly approaching, and no cash, she was stuck. I offered the use of my credit card for the deposit on car seats because she promised to return them the following week. I found out later she sold them at a pawn shop to get gas money for the car. That chance encounter cost me more than $200, but dozens of other times the people always responded with thank you notes, follow-up e-mails, etc. Even with the occasional abuse, the more you give, the more you get in return.

Regardless of age, the best part of your life can always be ahead of you. I submit that with the right perspective and positive attitude, the best is yet to come—no matter how old you are. I also believe that facing our own death is easy in comparison to living life to its fullest. The hardest thing to do is muster up the courage it takes to face your real life and to give your personal best every day.

Life isn't about what *we* do; it's about what we do for others. In the long run, success is measured in how we have spent our time, talents, and treasures, how we invested in the future of our children, how we want to be known. In the end, how we are measured isn't the accumulation of earthly possessions or wealth, but instead what that wealth did for others.

Think about setting goals for becoming more socially responsible as you find success. What would you really like to contribute toward? Ultimately, it should be everyone's responsibility to give more than we take from our community and society. Is your contribution to society also in debt? One thing's for sure: If your life has purpose, then this account also must be in the black. Money alone isn't enough—not even close.

Quite often we need milestones—a big birthday, a health scare—to trigger the wake-up call. Is that the day that you will admit you need to plan or simplify your life? Maybe, or maybe not yet, so for now, keep a positive attitude regarding your destructive habits until you figure out how to slow down on the crazy stuff. After all, we must keep a good sense of humor about all the craziness. Just don't get to the point of snapping before you take action.

If you live under the influence of others who may not be giving you the best advice or that serve as enablers of your destructive habits, then it's time to stop and regain control of your own life. Likewise, if you live under the influence of an obsessive desire for material items or constant social connectivity, it's time for a change. Everyone has holes in their life. How we choose to fill them is of vital importance. Giving back and giving your best every day to something worthwhile is a great way to lead a more fulfilled life—a life very much worth living.

Life's most urgent question is: what are you doing for others?

Martin Luther King Jr.

○ ○ ○

Do you pass up opportunities to show human care in everyday situations?

_____

_____

_____

_____

Are you easily taken advantage of?

_____

_____

_____

_____

What else will you do to make the lives of those around you better?

_____

_____

_____

_____

Conclusion

All of this is so easy to say, yet so hard to do. Every idea I've written here is simple and, most times, obvious. Where and how to begin to make a change for the better is the difficult assignment if you attempt a total transformation. Instead, try a chapter at a time and focus on it for a month or two. Digging out of a hectic and unfulfilling life is a major life-changing experience and is very hard work. Small steps can lead to progress.

If you're not sure where to start, begin with your money situation. Read chapters 19 and 20, and if you have any of these financial woes mentioned, start here and make progress. Focusing here will make it easier to identify the things you need to give up. What do you have that you can't afford? What do you have that you can live without?

Young people, as a broad categorization, have developed a reputation for not having good common sense. I think it is in part because you have grown up with a "menu-driven" hierarchy for taking next steps and making decisions. In other words, your choices have been presented like a restaurant menu. You make the first choice, then the next, and then the next, until you find what you are looking for. But what guides you when these logical choices aren't available? That's the common sense, or street smarts, you need to hone.

My generation had to do its own research, use its own instincts, and solve problems from its own experiences. We couldn't just text our parents or use Wikipedia. Think about how a world of instant information at your fingertips may be causing you to skip an important step or two in gaining real knowledge. It goes back to the process, or journey. Skipping steps, not knowing the difference between information and knowledge, and having everything at your fingertips devalues experience and wisdom. This, combined with the habit of sending and receiving instantaneous responses, may be a social influence contributing to the lack of common sense argument.

As an employer, it is very common to have intelligent and hard-working employees that simply do not share your same core values. Those employees won't last long, and they shouldn't. If you commit to always doing the right thing, no matter the cost, the results seem to take care of themselves. Encourage young people to be authentic, real, express themselves with emotion, and sincerely care.

As a Millennial, the secret to success is to define what you value most, surround yourself with those who share those same values, distance yourself from those who don't, and passionately live your values through every decision and action. When you do, you will look in the mirror with great pride and become envied by those who have yet to learn these simple lessons. Be kind! Make a difference!

Becoming a Mentor:
Tips and Techniques

The secondary purpose for this book is to support a mentoring program within your organization. Few small businesses have a formal new employee orientation program much less offer mentorship opportunities for new hires. The mentoring concept has been around a long time, but getting formal programs established is fairly new.

You don't have to be in senior management or the owner of the company to get the ball rolling. A mentoring program developed from the top down shows the new employees a willingness to invest in them. A program created from the desire of the newer employees demonstrates to management a willingness to engage sooner in their development. In either case, the concept is simple and the potential value is huge.

- Mentors help the newer employees set career goals and start taking steps to realize them.
- Mentors can share the company culture and tell stories as examples.

- Mentors can be an inspiration for what the new hires can accomplish.
- Mentors can use their industry contacts to help young people meet other industry professionals, find success earlier, and explore more possibilities in their position.
- Mentors can provide their mentees with confidence in their decision making and overcome the fear of failure.
- Mentors introduce young people to company resources and outside organizations they may not know about.
- Mentors can help their mentees learn how to seek promotion and keep jobs.
- Mentors can help because they are supportive, not judgmental.

Recommendation: Before diving in and starting a mentoring program, carefully evaluate the following steps. These steps have been adapted for business use and are based upon the effective practices for mentoring from MENTOR, a not-for-profit organization that has given me permission to present their program model. I encourage you to visit www.mentoring.org for more details. Their mission is to establish youth mentoring programs, but the following steps can apply to workplace programs as well.

Step 1: Program Goals

Companies should develop a plan or guideline to define the overall goals of a mentoring program. The plan should address an organizational structure and benchmarks. Consider having an incentive program for mentors and mentees to encourage participation. This could be as simple as a recognition event or offering some form of financial reward for completing a predetermined length of engagement. The program should be endorsed at all levels, clear to the top of the organization, and be recognized often at company meetings and functions.

Step 2: Training

The mentors' program has many facets of training. The highly successful programs place a strong emphasis on training in order to develop consistency and quality of the mentors. I suggest you model your training program after other successful business-focused mentor programs in your area. Most not-for-profit organizations are willing to share this structural information. Even though they serve a very different audience, the training methods developed by local youth outreach agencies can serve as an effective model.

Step 3: Recruitment

Recruiting new mentees is a challenging step. Most companies find it harder to get young people into the program than to find mentors willing to participate. Finding the right match of mentor and mentee based on goals is important. Make sure you don't rush into the program before the right mentors are available that match the purpose for the program. It's best to wait and do it right from the outset with the right people in place. It has to be a positive outcome for the mentee each and every time.

Step 4: Screening

Not everyone makes a good mentor or mentee. This really has to be something a person truly believes in for them to get or give as much out of it as possible. Typically, the mentor achieves their satisfaction from imparting wisdom, sharing stories, and helping mentees avoid the mistakes they made. It can be very rewarding when mentors feel a sense of accomplishment from others' growth and success as they did their own. From a mentee standpoint, this has to be more than a guilt trip or a required activity. The mentees need to be serious about what the program offers them. Some programs go so far as to require an essay for admission or acceptance. It doesn't hurt to have a limited number of seats available and develop a sense of exclusivity to get into the program.

Step 5: Matchmaking

Teaming up people in accordance to personality type and level of maturity is important. It might be that you want to go outside the department of the mentee and rotate in other experienced mentors to cross-train, offering a perspective of the full scope of the organization. Mentoring is more about the right match for sharing experiences with behavioral and cultural matters than learning about products or services offered.

Step 6: Ongoing Support

These programs need to have a champion within the organization, and that person should closely monitor the progress and outcomes. It might be best to have a start and stop period, say six months or a year-long program. This way, it gives definition and closure to everyone involved. My experience tells me that when seeking volunteers, having specific roles and duties along with a timeframe for their service gets more people interested. The best mentors can sign on for additional terms, and those who didn't enjoy the experience can gracefully bow out when they finish.

Program modification should be expected once the first session concludes. It will become apparent which people enjoy and have the patience for this type of role and which ones don't. Additional training and resources for the program may need to be identified and made available from the program support person or organizer. The support person for the program should have a close connection to your Human Resources department and be well-versed in company policy. The mentors should also be trained for the correctness of their coaching as it relates to company HR policies.

Acknowledgments

Thanks to all of the following people who have in some fashion contributed to this book:

Authors and contributors to the NSCA BizSkills 3rd edition, including Brad Nelson, Todd Lucy, and Jeanne Stiernberg for their work on the original soft skills training manual.

Amanda Rooker, my editor, for her expertise and advice.

David Hancock, my publisher, for taking the time and effort to work with me.

My friends Jay Myers, Mike Hester, Ron Pusey, and Mike Bradley for encouraging me to write this book.

Members of the NSCA Board of Directors and the NSCA Education Foundation for their support of this project.

Current and former NSCA employees and their commitment to always doing things the right way.

Members of NSCA and the electronics systems industry that have allowed me to observe, mentor, coach, and consult them in their businesses.

Former students and student athletes that I've had the privilege to teach and coach and, most importantly, learn from. Those experiences were priceless.

About the Author

Charles "Chuck" Wilson is an internationally recognized technology and business development expert. He serves as the CEO and Executive Director for the National Systems Contractors Association (NSCA), a not-for-profit organization representing the world's leading technology providers. In 1999, Chuck founded the NSCA Education Foundation, whose mission is to assist young technology professionals in getting started in their career. He was also a founding member of the Electronic Systems Professional Alliance (ESPA), an organization that helps provide training and certification programs for college graduates as they enter the workforce.

Chuck speaks on a wide range of business topics, including the effective use of technology and developing a world-class workforce. He has been published in hundreds of journals, books, and leading trade magazines, and publishes his own weekly blog. He has run a small business, served on numerous charitable organizations boards, and volunteered as a school board chairman, coach, and technology instructor. He lives in Cedar Rapids, Iowa, with his wife Pam and their two dogs. His son Austin is a student at the University of Iowa.

Proceeds from the sale of this book will be used
to benefit the NSCA Education Foundation

NSCA EDUCATION
FOUNDATION

About the NSCA Education Foundation

The NSCA Education Foundation exists to promote and advance the electronic systems industry by offering pathways for career development. We provide scholarships and awards to assist existing professionals and those pursuing careers within the electronic systems integration industry. We are committed to the growth of the industry by providing access to the best education and latest techniques available.

The electronic systems integration industry is a community comprised of individuals with a passion for technology, constantly striving to showcase technologies and applications in unique and exciting marketplaces. This high-tech industry is rapidly growing with many opportunities for a rewarding career.

In 1999, the association which advocates for the electronic systems integrator – the National Systems Contractors Association (NSCA), led by their CEO Chuck Wilson – formed this education foundation with the sole purpose of focusing on the personal growth of the people working within the industry, as well as to recruiting new people to join the profession.

As a 501(c) (3) charitable organization, the NSCA Education Foundation raises funds through sponsorships of special events and contributions members of the systems integration industry in order to provide access to the best education and training programs available.

The NSCA Education Foundation promotes and engages current and future electronic systems integrators in educational experiences to enhance the growth, professionalism and business skills needed in the electronic systems industry. One of our unique initiatives is to create and promote industry networking and mentoring opportunities within our industry.

For more information on the NSCA Education Foundation or mentorships, visit www.nscafoundation.org.

Printed in the USA
CPSIA information can be obtained
at www.ICGtesting.com
JSHW082345140824
68134JS00020B/1895